Breaking the
Ten Commandments

Discover the Deeper Meaning

Eric Butterworth

Also by Eric Butterworth

Spiritual Economics

Discover the Power Within You

In the Flow of Life

Unity: A Quest for Truth

Celebrate Yourself! And Other Inspirational Essays

Life Is for Living

Life Is for Loving

The Concentric Perspective: What's in It From Me

*The Universe Is Calling: Opening to the Divine
Through Prayer*

Breaking the
Ten Commandments

Discover the Deeper Meaning

Eric Butterworth

Unity Village, MO 64065-0001

Breaking the Ten Commandments
Softcover Edition 2011

Unity Books titles are available at special discounts for bulk purchases for study groups, book clubs, sales promotions, books signings or fundraising. To place an order, call the Unity Customer Care Department at 1-866-236-3571 or email *wholesaleaccts@unityonline.org.*

Breaking the Ten Commandments was originally published by Unity School of Christianity under the title *MetaMorality: A Metaphysical Approach to the Ten Commandments.* (This book was formerly published by Harper & Row, Publishers, Inc., under the title *How to Break the Ten Commandments.*)

Acknowledgment is made to Harcourt Brace Jovanovich, Inc., and to Faber and Faber Ltd., publishers of *The Complete Poems and Plays of T. S. Eliot,* for permission to reprint lines from *The Cocktail Party* by T. S. Eliot.

The Bible references, unless otherwise indicated, are from the Revised Standard Version, copyright 1946 (renewed 1973), 1952 and © 1971 by the Division of Christian Education of the National Council of the Churches of Christ in the U.S.A.

Cover design: Mark Szymanski, Senior Multimedia Artist, Unity
Interior design: The Covington Group, Kansas City, Missouri

Library of Congress Control Number: 87-82241
ISBN: 978-0-87159-339-9
Canada BN 13252 9033 RT

To Olga,
my beautiful helpmate
for her loving support and
indispensable collaboration
of the Spirit

"No man-made law is strong enough, or true enough, or exact enough to be a permanent guide for anyone."

—Charles Fillmore, *The Twelve Powers*

CONTENTS

FOREWORD

I was introduced to the writing of Eric Butterworth early in my career as a Truth student. His books influenced me more powerfully than those of any other writer. Tape recordings of his lectures played constantly on my car stereo. I listened to Butterworth tapes as I drove cross country in a rented truck loaded with all my worldly goods to begin preparing for ordination as a Unity minister.

Years later I would meet Butterworth when he attended a seminar I presented at a Unity conference about computer software for Bible study. I enjoyed meeting with him in his office at the Unity Center, and addressing his congregation at Avery Fisher Hall in New York City. I still reference the notes I made when, for two days in the late 1990s, he addressed the ministerial students at Unity Institute®, where I serve as a member of the faculty. Now, as the host of *Discovering Eric Butterworth* on Unity Online Radio, it's my privilege to introduce Butterworth and his work to a new generation of Truth students, and to help some of his former students rediscover the work of this great teacher, author and Unity minister.

This book first drew my attention with the unusual title of its first edition: *How to Break the Ten Commandments*. Leave it to Eric Butterworth, I thought, to come up with a new perspective on one of the most ancient teachings of Western religion. Even people outside the Judeo-Christian tradition are aware of the Ten Commandments. Many of us learned about them in Sunday School and wondered why teachers never offered a clear answer when we asked what "committing adultery" and "coveting" meant. We learned all the "thou shalts" and "thou shalt nots," and that was about it. When asked how the Ten Commandments can serve as an effective guide for people in today's world, how many of us can offer an explanation that makes sense?

Butterworth would very likely agree with a description of his spiritual insights as iconoclastic, or "image-breaking." He had little use for outer forms, considering them barriers to deeper understanding. About the Ten Commandments, he writes: "If we could break through the crystallized shell of the Decalogue, we would discover some marvelous guidelines for the integrated life." In *Breaking the Ten Commandments: Discover the Deeper Meaning,* Butterworth really does "break through" the archaic language we find in traditional presentations of the Ten Commandments. With daring insight, he leads the reader to the essence—literally the "beingness," the vital energy—that has always been waiting to be discovered within this ancient teaching.

Here, as in his other works, Butterworth focuses on *you,* the reader, on *your* life, *your* concerns, *your* spiritual evolution. In *Breaking the Ten Commandments: Discover the Deeper Meaning,* you'll find provocative questions like:

- Do you believe in God? Or do you think that by saying you believe in God you really believe?
- What are some of the "graven images" we hold in place of true God awareness today?
- How often do we "take God's name in vain" and not even realize we're doing it?
- What is good?
- What is the Sabbath day and how can we keep it holy?
- How can we "honor our father and mother" if our relationship with our parents has been difficult or painful?
- How can we honor the spirit of the commandment "Thou shalt not kill" in a world where we witness so much violence?
- Whenever we see less than the Christ in another or in ourselves, we commit adultery. Does this thought surprise you?
- What is, in the long run, the only way to overcome the tendency or even the temptation to look for shortcuts to acquisition or achievement?
- Why is it true that we are actually incapable of "bearing false witness"?

- How can we reclaim the energy we have tied up in "covetousness" or envying others' possessions and achievements, and use that energy in a positive way?

As I read *Breaking the Ten Commandments: Discover the Deeper Meaning* again in preparing to write this foreword, I reconnected with some of my favorite "Butterworthisms." I recognized that I had first discovered many of the stories, illustrations and Truth insights I've used again and again in my own speaking and teaching in this powerful book. I pray, affirming that you, whether you're opening this volume for the first time or well beyond the hundredth time, will find both inspiration and practical guidance as you continue on your spiritual path.

Namaskar!

Tom Thorpe
Unity Minister and Instructor and Subject Matter Expert in Unity Institute
Unity Village, Missouri

August 30, 2010

INTRODUCTION

The world stands out on either side
No wider than the heart is wide;
Above the world is stretched the sky,
No higher than the soul is high.
The heart can push the sea and land
Farther away on either hand;
The soul can split the sky in two,
And let the face of God shine through.

These lines of Edna St. Vincent Millay's poem "Renascence" are both sobering and heartening as a perspective for viewing the contemporary world. They seem to say that the world we live in is about as big as we are, and the problems of the world come from our own limited faith and ideals.

But she also points to the Truth that we are never further away from transcendental solutions than the thought of God. We may be worried about the morality of our society and the integrity of people; but it is not a godless society, and the integrating power of God is within every person as the key to growth and change.

In a day that has produced Watergate and Iran-Contra debacles in our nation's capital, and insider trading scandals on Wall Street, it is not uncommon to hear the call to get back to religion, back to God. I am not sure I know what this means. If it means getting back to moralistic preaching and piously professing clichés, I am less than enthusiastic. But if it means a renewed effort to "split the sky in two, and let the face of God shine through" within each person is an awareness that not only improves conduct and changes character, but also modifies consciousness, then I say, "Amen!"

A letter to the editor of the local paper touches on the theme, "If people would just live by the Ten Commandments, we would have honesty and integrity in business and personal relationships and peace in the world." Certainly the Ten Commandments of the Judeo-Christian Bible form the backbone of the religion of hundreds of millions of people. Unquestionably the Ten Commandments have influenced the development of modern civil law in the Western world. But who knows them, or actually lives by them?

The phrase "The Ten Commandments" has become the "great cliché" of Western religion. Often it is used as an excuse for noninvolvement with the religious establishment: "Oh, I don't go to church. I just live by the Ten Commandments. What more can one do?" Yet how many persons who parrot the cliché could repeat even five of the commandments?

Or locate them in the Bible? Or even have a Bible in their homes?

We have been taught to *keep* the commandments, and we have kept them all too well. We have enshrined them like religious relics in sealed containers on the altar. Thus, it could be said that one lives *by* the commandments in much the same way as many persons live *by* a neighbor, never learning his name, let alone having any understanding communication with him.

If Jesus was anything, he was an iconoclast, breaking with the traditions of the past, and giving emphasis to the "practice of the Presence" in the present. He sets a tone that clearly indicates his belief in the need for every individual to break down the tablets of stone so as to find in them a workable formula for victorious living. He said: *Ye have heard that it was said by them of old time ... but I say unto you ...* (Mt. 5:21, ASV).

Undoubtedly, a widespread commitment to the Truth of the Ten Commandments could touch off a great spiritual renaissance in the world today. But this could happen only if there were a mass commitment to the breakup of what Gilbert and Sullivan call "platitudes in stained-glass attitudes." If we could break through the crystallized shell of the Decalogue, we would discover some marvelous guidelines for the integrated life. How great is the need in our society for spiritually integrated people!

The religious world is rife with clichés. The Ten Commandments is only one. Michelangelo's masterwork on the ceiling of the Sistine Chapel has helped to create another. It is the stereotype of God as a man. True, it is a big man, a powerful man, a majestic and wise figure of a man, but still a man, with all the possibilities of wrath and capriciousness. Cecil B. DeMille made skillful use of this cliché in the motion picture *The Ten Commandments*, which is thus a grossly misleading caricature. For though we do not actually see the big man "out there," we hear the booming voice of wrath and we see the "work of his hands."

Paradoxically, the commandments themselves are intended to turn us from this very kind of distorted imagery. The hand of God etching the commandments on tablets of stone is cinematography at its best and communication at its worst. For it completely misses the symbolism that is so important to understand the narrative of Moses' spiritual experience. It totally misses the full meaning of Mt. Sinai.

For generations Bible researchers have tried in vain to locate Mt. Sinai, the high mountain on which Moses is supposed to have received the tablets of stone from God. Perhaps they have been looking in the wrong place. Charles Fillmore defines *Sinai* metaphysically as a "high or exalted state of consciousness." Because of the cliché of the big man "out there," we repeatedly lose the sense of infinite Mind "in whom we live and move and have our being." In the account of Moses' wilderness experience, he seems to say, "You don't have to go anywhere to get into infinite Mind." For at the burning bush, he records hearing a voice from within, saying: *"Put off your shoes from your feet, for the place on which you are standing is holy ground"* (Ex. 3:5).

It is important to recall that Moses came to Mt. Sinai after many years of spiritual development in the wilderness of Horeb. During this period there evolved within him a strong awareness of the omnipresence of God, and of man's oneness with "the One." All else in the Sinai story must be seen against this backdrop. In his inner search for ways to help his people to find their freedom, he perceived that the causes of their suffering were in their attitudes and sense of values. His goal was to bring them into an awareness of "the Lord our God is One" (the Jewish Shema). These were undeveloped people, thus, in an experience of cosmic perception (Mt. Sinai), he evolved a set of guidelines that were designed to meet their needs at the level of their ability to comprehend.

Look carefully at the commandments. It appears that they are restrictive laws set down by fiat of the divine dictator. Surely they seem to be careful lines of conduct by which the Israelites *must* live. However, law is not coercive but supportive. The commandments were (and are) fences to keep the undeveloped ones from wandering. Children need fences, and teenagers may need curfews and times of "grounding." But there must come a time when they "put away childish things" and move on toward maturity and self-reliance.

When dealing with gravity, a child must be told, "Don't lean out the window; don't get too close to the well." As he matures, he understands gravity's inexorable function, and so the parent's commandment ceases to be coercive and punitive. For gravity is supportive, holding him in his chair as he sits, enabling him to walk and run and jump and play. Thus, abiding on the right side of the law of gravity becomes second nature to him as he goes about the business of living.

The Ten Commandments are usually considered to be the basis for morality. However, morality deals not with spiritual law, but with "accepted rightness." Recent history has revealed dramatically that it is a short step to the rationalization that "everyone is doing it." The great need of every person is to understand his inherent spiritual nature, and thus that it is not a matter of what is being done, but what is the very best he can do. It is not enough to be superior to other persons; we should strive to be superior to our former selves. Beyond morality is a whole new dimension of metamorality. It is the deeper meaning in the Ten Commandments.

Religious institutions often engage in image-making. The emphasis is on the good reputation, or moral uprightness, which may be equated with being seen going to church, kneeling or standing at the correct moment in the service, joining in the public recitation of the commandments and other religious codes by rote. Religion might achieve a new public acceptance if the "good life" were to be measured not by the way we conform to religious codes, but by the degree to which we live by what Thornton Wilder calls "the incredible standard of excellence." This is what metamorality is all about. It is what this book is about.

Religious education has made great strides in recent years. However, all too often it still consists of rote-learning of custom-made convictions. Parents want Johnny to have a "good religious background." He is sent off regularly to "school" where he learns the Ten Commandments and an assortment of creeds under rigid discipline and holy threats of eternal punishment. All this is directed toward the important time of confirmation or bar mitzvah. There is a great occasion of joy and celebration and a collective sigh of relief. Now Johnny is a card-carrying member of the religious community, which he proves not necessarily by attendance at services, but always by stating the great cliché, "I live by the Ten Commandments."

This is not to denigrate the fundamental Truths that inhere in all the great religions of the world, or the need to build lives on laws of living such as outlined in the Ten Commandments. However, man is not a plaything of the gods, nor even of God. Man is a spiritual being, alive and living within a universal system that is constantly supportive. The idea of keeping God's commandments to honor Him, and thus to accept certain restraints set down "for some inscrutable reason of His own," may be extremely confusing to most persons.

The goal of this book is not to herald the Ten Commandments in their literal or crystallized form, but rather to break them down, one by one, to their underlying esoteric meaning. I am confident that you will discover some understandable spiritual fundamentals that will open new vistas of growth and unfoldment for you.

Perhaps I should emphasize that each commandment deals with a spiritual insight relatable to life on many levels. You may want to come back to specific chapters again and again, using the ideas as a basis for meditation. The object is to break through the limited states of consciousness that may have held you in bondage, like the Israelites of old. May this book be as a Moses unto you to help you go forward, through your own wilderness of spiritual growth, into your Promised Land of spiritual fulfillment and human achievement.

Metamorality is an idea whose time has come. It could be a powerful instrument in bringing light and effectiveness into all the many well-meaning attempts to create a moral climate in our schools, our business community, and in our political system. Don't be bashful in bringing its message to the world. But keep a balance by remembering, "Let there be peace (integrity, honesty, fair play) on earth, and let it (them) begin with me."

The
FIRST
Commandment

I am the Lord your God, who brought you out of the land of Egypt, out of the house of bondage. You shall have no other gods before me (Ex. 20:2-3).

The first commandment presents us with an immediate crisis of understanding. For if we view these words as religious tradition has interpreted them, the mind runs inescapably toward billowy clouds, a regal throne, a majestic figure with a long, white beard and a booming voice calling out, "I am the one, and you had better believe it!"

Let me forewarn you. Unless you can break out of this shell of ignorance and let go the belief in the big man "out there," then the rest of this book will be of little meaning to you. This first chapter is the great test. Unless you can successfully break open this first commandment, the remaining nine will remain inviolable.

Shocking as it may seem, the "God of our fathers" is no longer adequate. Life in the space age calls for a larger thought of God. Ralph Waldo Emerson realized this many years ago when he startled audiences with the suggestion that when we break with our God of tradition and cease from the God of our intellect, God will fire the heart with His presence.

Do you believe in God? Or do you think that by saying you believe in God you really believe? To really believe in God is to have a sense of the wholeness of life and of the universe, which in turn gives rise to a believing attitude. Do you believe in yourself? Do you believe in people? Do you believe in life as a meaningful experience? If not, then your God is little more than a three-letter word, and your "I believe in God" an empty cliché.

"Hear, O Israel: The Lord our God is one Lord; and you shall love the Lord your God with all your heart, and with all your soul, and with all your might" (Deut. 6:4-5). This is the most important scripture taught to Jewish children, and it has always been the confession of faith among the Jews. It is the lovely Shema, which contains an insight that is vital to the meaning of the first commandment: THE ONE. It is the basic unity on which all things are built. The ancients wisely

directed people to behold but one in all things, for it is the second that leads one astray.

The traditional concept of God has portrayed Him as living *in* the universe and acting *on* the forces of the universe. This has often implied a struggle with things and conditions of evil intent, sometimes even suggesting that He was having a hard time of it. A preacher once cried out, "We are here today to unite in support of our God. He has a great battle on His hands with the devil, and if He fails it will be the end of all of us!" What an anemic concept of the universal process!

To have no other gods before THE ONE is to have the awareness of the allness of God. God is the allness in which the whole of the universe and all that is in it exist as manifestations. Whatever the universe is, it exists within the allness which is God. Thus "the Creator" does not mold and shape things and set them "down here" to fend for themselves. He (or It) can only be understood as a process that acts upon and within itself to manifest as stars, atoms and people. Thus every person is an eachness within the allness that is God.

You are the very activity of God expressing as you. To creatively believe *in* God, then, is to believe *from* the consciousness *of* God. This believing energy is the continuation of the divine process that made you in the first place. This is why faith is such a tremendous creative power.

When faith is limited to the cliché of "faith in God," there is a tendency to accommodate the second that leads one astray. In other words, we have many gods within the framework of our belief system. We may believe in God ... and the devil. We may believe in life ... and sickness. We may believe in substance ... and lack. And how we worship at the altars of the medicine cabinet, the great good luck charms, and the unemployment compensation!

You may think you believe in God, but do you believe *from* the allness of God? Or does your faith waver between God as substance and your waning dividends, between God as health and the corner drugstore, between God as your guide and the daily horoscope?

If all things exist *in* and have being out of the all-ness of God, how can there be any other power? If the principle is 2 plus 2 equals 4, how can there be a force that tempts us to get 3? The doctrine of evil as a power, and of Satan as the prince of darkness, is a blight upon true religion. It is a rationalistic philosophy that evolved out of our inability to understand or justify human experience, and the attempt to find a scapegoat. Without a realistic understanding of the first commandment, we ask, "How could God permit the good religious person to suffer so?" Or, "Why would God cause the tragic earthquake that destroyed so much life and property?" But to even ask the question implies that we have not made the breakthrough to the inner meaning of the commandment, "The Lord our God is one Lord."

Human problems are not in God but in our limited awareness of God. Under the Pythagorean system of mathematics, all numbers proceed from unity and are resolvable back again into unity. All things begin with "1." We can duplicate "1" and have "2" or "99" or a million. We can create complicated problems and formulas, but all are resolvable back again into the basic "1." Perhaps, if we had a full knowledge of the "1," which is essential unity, we would know all that exists in the world and we would have no further need for mathematics. This presupposes much, but it also tells us much of the importance of "1."

The basic ONE in the process of manifestation becomes "I AM." Much has been written about the "great I AM," usually complicating a simplicity instead of simplifying a complexity. I AM is simply *being* in the process of *being you*. Thus, it is significant that the first commandment begins with *"I am the Lord your God."* This means that "I AM is the Lord of your being." Only you can say "I AM." It is your true identity. It is the Presence of God in you, being you.

The mission of Moses was based on the dramatic revelation to him of the divine name. Tending sheep in the wilderness, he had a cosmic experience in the form of a vision of leading his people out of their bondage in Egypt. The human of him cried out, "But who shall I say sent me?" It was a natural human reaction: "How can I do such a thing?" But out of the depths of his inner being came the realization, *"I AM has sent me to you"* (Ex. 3:14). It was the first breakthrough into cosmic consciousness that ultimately led to the Ten Commandments. However, it is important to realize that the commandments did not come forth as divine edicts, but as carefully worked out guidelines for integrative living. The same cosmic perception that revealed the "I AM" led to the understanding to present the laws of life in the form and at the level of consciousness that Moses' people could relate to.

Under Moses' inspired leadership some pretty dramatic things were done by the power of the name "I AM." Unfortunately, the people did not understand the powerful implications. For generations the legacy of Moses was limited to a rigid code that was never completely unlocked. The key to Moses' law was the "I AM." In the centuries later, the key to understanding Jesus' teaching is the same "I AM." He said that he did not intend to destroy the law but to fulfill it, but he made it very clear that he intended to break the code.

It is significant that there is no predicate for the "I AM." This has caused many problems for those who have tried to understand the words without insight into the code. To predicate anything implies a special aspect of it, thus implying limits. It is not possible to apply a limiting predicate to the ONE, the allness of God, for there can be nothing outside of it.

People did not understand Jesus when he said: *"I am the way, and the truth, and the life"* (Jn.14:6) and *"I am the resurrection and the life"* (Jn.11:25). They thought that God was being predicated as Jesus, and that Jesus, thus, had a special dispensation of power.

How biblical translation has confused this issue! A case in point: John 8:24. The various authorized versions of the Bible render this: "Except you believe that I am *he*, you will die in your sins." The italics indicate that the "he" has been a problem. When we consult the "Emphatic Diaglott," the line-by-line translation from the Greek, we can see why, for it clearly indicates that there is no "he" in the original. It was obviously added "for clarity," for it seemed to call for a predicate. This addition has had a profound influence on Christian theology. It has been made to appear that Jesus was saying that there is no hope for humanity unless we believe that "I am God." Actually, He was saying, "Unless you get this conviction of the basic ONE, the I AM awareness, you are bound in your consciousness of limitation, which will inevitably lead to deterioration and death."

Jesus did not come to tell of his divinity, making him the great exception. His whole mission was to help us to know of our own divinity, and to make of himself an example of the "I AM" coming to full personal expression in us. The tragedy is that tradition has made Jesus a God and worshiped him. Thus for most Christians the code remains unlocked. The key is very simply: *Ye shall know the truth, and the truth shall make you free* (Jn. 8:32 ASV).

Know the ONE, the Allness of God, and you will always be in the flow of good. No evil will befall you and you will find peace in all your ways. This is the message of the Bible, repeated again and again, in parable and allegory and psalm. One good example is the story of King Nebuchadnezzar and the "fiery furnace."

The King of Babylon had issued an edict that people must worship an idol of gold he had set up on the Plain of Dura. The penalty for infraction of the rule was severe: death in a furnace of fire. Now "certain Jews" (Shadrach, Meshach and Abednego) refused to bow down before the idol, and thus they were summarily thrown into the furnace. But amazingly, they came out unscathed, without even the smell of fire on their clothes. Nebuchadnezzar relented and commanded that all people should worship Jehovah, "the ONE."

Like the Ten Commandments, the entire Bible must be broken down so that its underlying message may be revealed. While outwardly it is a book of history and of morals, inwardly it is an outline of spiritual Truths and dealing with one very important person ... you. The Israelites symbolize the ascending urge within you. Their temptation to worship false gods relates to the harassment that you may often feel by "the second that leads one astray." Characters like Nebuchadnezzar represent the human tendency to judge by appearances. It is that within you that says, "You might as well face the facts that this situation is hopeless." It is this negative function of the mind that may throw you into the furnace of fire, the turmoil of mental and emotional upset.

You may consider yourself to be a good student of this "new insight in Truth." You may feel that you are well-grounded in the awareness of the allness of God and the omnipresence of this God-activity in every part of your life. And then one Friday afternoon your employer hands you your paycheck, which includes a little yellow slip that says, "Your services are no longer required." You may go through your disciplined drill, "I have faith that all things work together for my good. God is my all-providing sub-stance and supply," etc.

But then old Nebuchadnezzar, the part of you that is "practical," says, "Look, at your age no one wants you. You are in for some real problems!" Down on your knees you go before the god of lack! There may be a tendency to go running after many gods by using the "I AM" power in negative ways: "I am afraid; I am worried; I am at the end of my rope." And yet, if you hold to the Truth, like Shadrach, Meshach and Abednego, you will come through the turmoil without even the smell of fire on your person.

This is not to minimize the problems of life, but rather to maximize the power of the principle. Problems of arithmetic are to be faced. But within every problem there is an answer, because the prob-lem, no matter how complex, exists within the prin-ciple. The complexity of the numerical forms is com-pletely reducible back into the basic "1." There is no point in saying that the evil condition does not exist. The injustice and the pain and the loss may be all too apparent. But evil is not a spiritual reality. It is simply a changing mental aberration, a concealment of the basic good. The sinfulness of a person is simply the frustration of his divine potential. He may long have frustrated it, and he may continue to frustrate it, but it remains his potential. This is the spark we might desecrate but never quite lose. It is *Christ in you, the hope of glory* (Col. 1:27). It is every person's hope of overcoming.

One may be faced with a need for healing, but confused about how to approach it. The illness is there all right, and it is not negative to see it and accept it as a condition to be met. The condition is not outside of God. Rather, it is a frustration within the life of God. Allness remains the reality. There is allness even within the illness. This is the basic key to healing, the assurance that the person *can* be healed because he *is* whole.

Note how, when Jesus stood at the tomb of Lazarus, He prayed the prayer of ONENESS. He did not give in to appearances and say, "I am sorry folks, it is too late!" He did not plead with God to work a miracle. He simply "lifted up his eyes" to turn from the appearance, and returned in consciousness to the principle, "I am the resurrection and the life." This was to state the principle, to know the Truth, and to affirm oneness with the ONE.

How could Jesus be so sure? Why is the mathematician so sure, so confident in the principles of mathematics? Because they *are* principle. He would never think of accusing the principle of mathematics for errors in computation. It never occurred to Jesus to trace the death of Lazarus to God. Others might have done so, but not Jesus. He said: *"It is not the will of my Father ... that one of these little ones should perish"* (Mt. 18:14).

Principle *is* principle, not caprice. It is universal and inexhaustible. In principle every person is an eachness within the allness of God. This means that you are God expressing *as* you. It was Jesus' great discovery: the divinity of humanity. It was the direction of Moses' work to lay the foundation of the move from personality to principle. This is what the Ten Commandments are all about.

In our quest for Truth we are dealing with personal growth and self-realization. It is not a matter of trying to get into God or to get God into us. Rather, it is "be still, and know that I am God." The shadows of human experience indicate that in one way or another our God-self is being concealed. We are standing in our own shadows, and then fretting that they are outside forces. We need to say, much as Jesus did, "Get thee hence, for there is but one God, and God only will I serve."

How do you serve God? There is only one way: by believing that you *deserve* His total and complete support. Jesus said: *"It is your Father's good pleasure to give you the kingdom"* (Lk. 12:32). It *is*, not was or will be or "dear Lord let there be."

Thus, the whole idea of worship of God needs to be broken down into the basic realization of "The One." Teilhard de Chardin, in his *Divine Milieu*, refers to the presence that Emerson says we experience when we have "broken with the god of tradition." He says: *The presence is so universal and we are so surrounded and transfixed by it—there is no room to fall down and adore it, even within ourselves.*

What a freeing insight this is! For we have tried to worship God, much as Nebuchadnezzar commanded people to worship the golden idol. The word *worship*, from the Greek *proskuneo*, means "to fawn or crouch, to prostrate oneself in homage." As long as we hold the man-out-there image in consciousness, our worship will be an act of self-abasement. But when we break with that concept, actually break the first commandment, then we know that God is not a person to approach in servility, but a principle and process to express in expanded consciousness. Praying to God is actually a "practice of the *absence* of God." The need is to return to the principle, "The One," and then pray *from* the consciousness *of* God. Instead of seeking to overcome God's reluctance, enlightened prayer seeks only to become attuned to His eternal supportiveness.

Jesus said: *"God is spirit, and those who worship him must worship in spirit and truth"* (Jn. 4:24). We worship God most effectively through the awareness and practice of *creative worth-ship*. It is the celebration of the I AMness of you, giving focus to the creative process within ... that it may flow forth through you.

Walt Whitman was called an egotist and an atheist, though he was surely neither. But he may have reflected the keenest insight into the nature of God, the purpose of life, and the spirit of true worship when he proclaimed, "I celebrate myself." Jesus said it in a slightly different way: *"I am the light of the world"* (Jn. 8:12), *"You are the light of the world. ...Let your light so shine"* (Mt. 5:14,16).

The first commandment is commended to you, but the next step is yours. Make a commitment today to "The One." Know that you are one with "The One" and in "The One." Do not give in to the human tendency to keep the commandment in terms of a phrase that so easily becomes a cliché. Break it down every day into an awareness of "The One," and make a daily commitment to live in that consciousness.

The
SECOND
Commandment

You shall not make yourself a graven image, or any likeness of anything that is in heaven above, or that is in the earth beneath, or that is in the water under the earth; you shall not bow down to them or serve them; for I the Lord your God am a jealous God, visiting the iniquity of the fathers upon the children to the third and fourth generation of those who hate me, but showing steadfast love to ... those who love me and keep my commandments (Ex. 20:4-6) .

This is one commandment that we can dispense with quickly as quite irrelevant to the Truth-seeker in modern times. Or so it would seem. For who of us today is seriously involved in the worship of idols? However, we think you will see that, when broken down to its essence, this second commandment is extremely relevant to each of us. Its implication is as vital as anything we may encounter, not only in all the Ten Commandments, but in all that we deal with in our quest for Truth.

The word *graven* means "carved," and thus the graven image referred to the figures of stone and gold and wood that have been central in the religious practices of pagan people of all cultures. Many have been the attempts to depict God or the gods in finite form: the African fetish, the Eskimo totem, the Egyptian dung beetle, the Phoenician Baal, the Hindu Kali, the many-breasted Diana of the Ephesians, and the all-too-human gods of the Greeks and Romans. But these are no longer an influence in our Western civilization. Of course, we could consider the Judeo-Christian use of icons, scrolls and statues as coming under the scope of the second commandment. However, as we will see, there are more important applications of a much more personal nature.

You may recall that when Moses returned from the mountain with the tablets of stone containing the Ten Commandments, he found his people engaged in a wild orgy of worship of a golden calf. In anger Moses threw the tablets to the ground and broke them into many pieces. The metaphysical implication is clear that stone tablets alone are insufficient to lead people to a higher way of life. They can so easily become graven images themselves, objects to give lip service to instead of principles to practice. So this act of Moses' breaking of the tablets seems to indicate that the stability of human life cannot be achieved by *keeping* the commandments alone, but only by breaking them down into their underlying spiritual essence.

As we noted in the first commandment, the fundamental principle is "I AM the Lord your God." This refers to the divine flow. Your life, your health, your love, your good ... all come through the creative flow pouring forth from within. You are a unique individualization of the divine flow. This is why Jesus, quoting from the Old Testament, emphasized the divinity of humanity: *"Is it not written in your law, 'I said, you are gods'?"* (Jn. 10:34).

However, like the Israelites of old, we have created our golden calves. The Preacher of Ecclesiastes puts it in an interesting way: *"God, when he made man, made him straightforward, but man invents endless subtleties of his own"* (Eccl. 7:29, NEB). And it is among these "endless subtleties" that we find the various forms of graven images.

In the beginning God ... These are the most important words of the Bible. The "in the beginning" means *in principle*. All things have their beginning in the principle of mind-action, the Infinite Creative

Process by which all things manifest. *God created man ... in the image of God he created him* (Gen. 1:27). Man is created in and of this Infinite Process, with the potential to continue the process in the unfoldment of his life and the works of his hands.

When man is spiritually integrated, his life unfolds in the divine flow, and all things work for good. But when he loses sight of oneness and begins to think about and deal with *two-ness*, he "invents endless subtleties of his own." He conjures up all sorts of forces that have origin in his own mind, but which become factors in his life. As the ancients put it, "The slave is busy making whips for his master."

Instead of integrating ourselves with the "I AM" center within, keeping ourselves "straightforward" with the divine flow, we add a predicate to the "I AM." We vest power in persons, things and beliefs, which then assert that power over us. All of which is to frustrate our own inner flow, which is the real sin. *Every kind of sin committed by man boils down to a kind of idolatry ... putting something before God.*

Graven images take many forms. The word God is a good example. It is a symbol intended to indicate the unnamable and unknowable. Yet we think that to know the name is to know God. One may say, "I love God," and think he has fulfilled his religious obligation. But the word *God* is an abstraction. How can you love a word? The person may only love the idea

of saying he loves God. *If anyone says, "I love God,"
and hates his brother, he is a liar* (1 Jn. 4:20). Maybe the
only way you can know what you believe is by how
you see yourself acting.

A window is created to be seen through. But if it is
allowed to get dusty and dirty, in time it will become
opaque. Now, instead of seeing through the window,
we can only look at the window. It becomes an object
instead of a medium. As the words and symbols of
religions evolve, in time we do not look to that to
which they point; we simply kneel in adoration at the
window, the cross, the altar or the word God.

This may explain the stress on breaking the first
commandment. The old idea of God needs to be broken down that you may experience the Presence.
When you get the feeling of oneness with the
Presence, you know that there is no way to get outside it. God is the root of your being, the life of your
life, the love of your love, the mind of your mind.
This consciousness cannot be achieved so long as
there is any kind of intermediary with God, or any
involvement with religious statues, relics, or even
pictures of Jesus. For these may all become graven
images.

Of course, we must be realistic. Man in his spiritual immaturity has always found the need to clothe
God in human form. The story is told of a little girl
who was crying in the night. Her mother came to her

room and said, "Don't cry, dear, God is right here with you." To which the little one replied, "But I want someone with skin on!"

Thus, the carved figures and pictures and medallions may be sincerely intended to comfort us and reassure us. They are symbols of the ever-present love of God. But how easily and how often we confuse the symbolic for the real. Thus we have graven images. The sad thing is that while we vest power in the image, we lose the sense of our own oneness with the power within ourselves. This is why Emerson longed for a "firsthand and immediate experience with God."

The Truth is: WHAT YOU ACKNOWLEDGE TO BE YOUR MASTER, TO THAT YOU ARE A SERVANT. This refers not just to things happening around you but to things that are established within you. It means attitudes, and this is what the commandments are about. It is as if the walls of your house of consciousness are a gallery displaying all the graven images that you have formed out of your prejudices and fears and complexes. As Jeremiah said: *"You pervert the words of the living God"* (Jer. 23:36). It is as if you actually carved these mental aberrations into stone figures that have, then, been ensconced with reverence in various alcoves of the mind. There they sit in regal splendor, asserting their power in many an unguarded moment.

Here are just a few of the most common graven images of the mind: "That's just the way he is"; "She is a weak character; what can you expect"; "You can't trust people anymore"; "Some people get all the breaks"; "With my luck"; "*They* never give the little guy a chance"; "For a person of my age"; "Because I was very sick as a child"; "Office politics"; "He will never make it, for he is a born loser," etc.

When you catch the idea, you might want to add to the list. It could be extremely revealing, and somewhat frightening. For these are the graven images or fixed attitudes that you may have carved into the very fabric of your subconscious mind. Within you is the unborn possibility of limitless life, and yours is always the privilege and the responsibility of giving birth to it. But as long as you acknowledge these things to be your master, you are failing to take responsibility for your life. You are frustrating your own divine potential.

If you are forever worrying about your finances, anxious about those who seem to be a threat to your position, or fearful that certain foods or conditions of the weather may be an upset to your health, then, as Jesus said, you are worshiping mammon. You are making graven images.

If you give power to good luck or bad luck, to the Dow Jones averages, what you read in the paper, the talk of the "virus going around," or the pious pronouncements of a psychic or seer, then you are bowing down to graven images.

If you give undue power to ailments or handicaps, you are making graven images. How common is it to refer almost tenderly to one's condition as "my arthritis," "my allergy," "my inferiority complex," "my penchant for failing." In many cases one may have identified with them (and *as* them) for so long that they have become almost as family altars before which one kneels faithfully in homage.

The commandment says: *"For I ... am a jealous God, visiting ... iniquity ... upon ... those who hate me"* (Ex. 20:5). Modern Bible scholarship tells us that the word should be *zealous*. In the Aramaic the words appear almost identical, though there is a wide disparity of meaning. A jealous God would be a human god who is emotional and vindictive. Zealous, on the other hand, connotes constant in activity, like the flow of current in an electric circuit.

The reference to God visiting iniquity on the children of the third and fourth generation of them who hate Him ... is a figure of speech that must be broken down. It is unfortunate that the image of the wrathful and vindictive God of much of the Old Testament has never really been seen for what it is: the evidence of the limitation of consciousness of Bible writers, and certainly not a realistic picture of God. No children are ever punished for the sins of their fathers.

We are not even punished for our own mistakes ... we are punished *by* them. The divine flow within, like electric current, is ever supportive; but it cannot be short-circuited without painful results. Visiting iniquity on the third and fourth generation simply makes clear that if we frustrate the divine flow today, we may be in for a continuity of that frustration in the times to come.

The word *hate* as used in this commandment ("those who hate me") has been a problem to Bible students. For instance, in Luke 14:26, Jesus said: *"If anyone comes to me and does not hate his own father and mother and wife and children and brothers and sisters ... he cannot be my disciple."* This seems strangely inconsistent with his own obvious love for his mother, and with his general teaching of love. There are modern sects that have made capital out of the literal implication of this statement, saying that people should abandon their parents and loved ones and follow a particular guru or "perfect master."

In the Aramaic root, the word *hate* means to cut off or separate. *Love,* on the other hand, means to hold in oneness. Jesus was referring to the need to become established in the discipline of Truth. He was concerned with those persons who make a graven image of certain relationships, becoming overly smothered in their love and dependent on their support. He was saying, "Know your oneness with the divine flow within you and let go of the tendency to lean on people."

Consistent with Bible teaching, this commandment clearly deals with the cosmic law. When you cut yourself off from the divine flow, you are vulnerable to what it calls "iniquity," which could refer to any of the multitude of human challenges "that flesh is heir to." (This is a cliché that is totally without validity, for it is not inheritance but cause and effect.) It also shows the other more supportive side of the law, the promise of *"steadfast love to ... those who love me and keep my commandments"* (Ex. 20:6). This important Bible Truth is most clearly articulated in Jesus' parable of the prodigal son, when the young man *"began to be in want"* (Lk. 15:13, 14) because he separated himself from the father and went out into the *"far country."* And when he said: *"I will arise and go to my father,"* he was soon back into the fold of his father's love in a veritable "eat, drink and be merry" evidence of the healing flow.

There is yet another important aspect of the graven images implied in the second commandment: the false attitudes we hold about ourselves. Paul referred to this as seeing ourselves in a mirror darkly. "It follows, as the night the day," that one with a positive self-image sees himself as capable and confident, and he tends to draw experiences and relationships commensurate with his self-evaluation. On the other hand, one with a poor self-image sees himself as weak and worthless. He underbids himself in the marketplace and experiences a continuity of injustices, bad breaks and heartbreaking problems.

Genesis says: *God created man in his own image.* It is a great Truth to take seriously. Make it real by affirming: *God created* me *in His own image.* You are God's image of man in the form of *you*. Affirm this often and the poor self-image will begin to fade away, to be replaced by a healthy awareness of your rightful place in the divine flow. You will have a growing confidence that you have been endowed with divine potential and the power to fulfill.

To be created in the image of God means that "in the beginning"(in principle) you were formed as an idea in Infinite Mind. You can never be less than the God-idea in expression. Because you live and move and have your being in Infinite Mind, you are endowed with creative power to form and shape things and to look upon them and say, "It is good." Paul referred to this image of God in you as *Christ in you, the hope of glory* (Col. 1:27). Christian tradition has mistakenly equated the Christ with Jesus. The Christ is the divine image in man, while Jesus is one who brought that image to full expression.

Jesus did say: *"He who has seen me has seen the Father"* (Jn. 14:9). But he meant, "The divinity you see in me is the evidence of God expressing through me."

He said, *"No one is good but God alone"* (Lk. 18:19). He was trying to make it crystal clear that the God-power that expressed in and through him is the same power that indwells every person. He kept his life in sharp focus, releasing the full potential of the divine image within, while most persons *"light a lamp and put it under a bushel"* (Mt. 5:15) and thus base their lives on the "endless subtleties" of human consciousness.

Self-image psychology has interested many persons in improving their personality by changing their self-image. It is an approach that has been helpful to many, but it is fraught with much self-delusion. Too often it deals with trying to change the image in the mirror, and suggesting the kind of image one may want there. This might lead to trying to be like someone else. But you can never be someone else, no matter how you admire or envy him.

No matter where you are in consciousness, or how poor your evaluation of yourself, you do not need a new self-image. What you need is to let go of the graven image of yourself that you have carved into the fabric of your subconscious mind, and to know and release your own divine image. It has never changed through all your life. It is that perfect idea of you formed in the mind of the Infinite.

You are a unique creature with the image of God stamped upon you. You may not be expressing it, but there is no one on earth quite like you. Your work is not to get a new self-image but to release your true God-image, to *open out a way whence the imprisoned splendor may escape* (Robert Browning, "Paracelsus"). As Meister Eckhart might put it, the need is to let God be God in you, and let God unfold *as* you.

You could conceivably change your self-image and become outgoing and friendly, while behind this pasted-on façade might be the same feeling of self-rejection you have tried to escape from. The problem has not been solved through glossing it over with a "new image." Actually, it could be that the new self-image is a graven image that might further frustrate the flow of your good.

Instead of trying to shape a self-image that conforms to the things or attributes you yearn for, how much better to know that your own divine image is ever seeking expression in you and as you. A beautiful statement of the Bible that is almost universally misunderstood is John 3:16 (ASV): *For God so loved the world, that he gave his only begotten Son.* Fundamental Christianity has insisted that this refers to Jesus. Meister Eckhart gives the clue to its meaning: God never begot but one son, but the eternal is forever begetting the only-begotten. There is that of every person that is begotten of many sources: his parents, heredity, the influences of his environment, the styles and trends of Madison Avenue, etc. The image thus projected in the person's life may be synthetically carved to form the personality that obscures the true son-of-God self within. But the "only-begotten son" is that which is begotten only of God, the divine pattern and the creative potential to express it. In other words, "God so loved you that He gave you that which is begotten only of Him."

In meditation, take time to get acquainted with the true you, that of you that is begotten only of God, created in His image-likeness. The endless subtleties and graven images of the mind will fade away into nothingness. Make your commitment to the spiritual ideal that is commended to you in the second commandment, perhaps in a way such as this:

I will remember that I am forever in the flow of God as my resource of life, love, substance and wisdom. I will not bow down before any other power over my life ... for I will know that there is only one presence and one power ... God, the good, omnipotent. I will keep myself in the awareness that God loves me with an everlasting love, and that in His supportive love, He has endowed me with the power and potential of divine sonship. And I will have a mighty faith that, when this God-image becomes my self-image, when the within of me shall become the without of me, then truly the Kingdom will have come, the divine will will have been done, in the earth of human experience as it is in the heaven of potentiality.

The
THIRD
Commandment

You shall not take the name of the Lord your God in vain; for the Lord will not hold him guiltless who takes his name in vain (Ex. 20:7).

I n a day when profanity and the use of the four-letter word have become almost a dialect of our language, it would seem that this commandment is timely and very much needed. However, though the use of God's name in profanity is considered immoral and blasphemous, the real problem goes much deeper. It would be good if people could learn to communicate without vulgarity; but it is much more important that they learn to communicate positively and creatively, which is what the third commandment is basically about.

The word *vain* is a mistranslation. The Aramaic root wood is *dagalootha*, which means in falsehood.

Thus the commandment should read, "You shall not take the name of the Lord your God falsely." In other words, the divine name is the great positive, and it should never be used in ways that are negative.

As we have discovered, the name of the Lord is "I AM." Moses' commitment to law began with his personal revelation of the name of God: "I AM WHO I AM." More literally this means self-existent one, or the potential in infinite being to *be* a manifest form. The "I AM" is impersonal and universal, but we personalize it when we say, "I am me." At the heart and root of all biblical teaching is the strong inference that there is within every one of us an unborn possibility of limitless life, and that ours is the privilege, through the creative use of the "I AM," of giving birth to it.

Many important keys to personal power have been obscured in the Bible through mistranslation. For instance, in Genesis 4:26 (ASV) we read: *Then began men to call upon the name of the Lord.* Through modern scholarship we now know that this should be, "Then began men to call themselves *by* the name of the Lord." What a difference! Where the old translation implied that they were begging help from an outside God, the great Truth that has been so long buried in dogma is that the people became aware of the "self-existent one" within themselves which they called into dynamic existence by speaking the great positive "I AM."

It is important that you catch the idea of the infinite supportiveness of the divine flow, and the inexorable function of spiritual law. There is no caprice involved in the third commandment. The Lord refers to "law." The commandment simply says that there is great power in the word of Truth, and that if you misuse the word or direct it in negative ways, you will have to "pay the piper."

It is strange how many persons feel that they can use formal prayers, partake of the rite of communion, and even voice affirmations and treatments, but that what they put into words at other times does not count. But there is no "king's X." Jesus said that we give account of every idle word. The subconscious mind does not discriminate. You may say, "But I didn't really mean that; I was just kidding." But the subconscious mind cannot take a joke. It does not know the difference between thoughts that are *casual* and those that are *causal*. What you voice in words reflects a state of consciousness, and consciousness is forever projecting itself into manifestation. It is a sobering thought. It is just not good sense to put into words something that you do not want to see manifest in your life.

Permissiveness is a word we hear much today, usually referring to treatment of young people.

Certainly, much harm is done to children when we do not instill in them an awareness of and respect for spiritual and moral law. However, it may be of greater concern that the parents of these same children are all too permissive in their speech, which is far more dangerous and destructive. Children may turn out all right anyway, because of their "imprisoned splendor" and the divine desire to unfold it. But verbal permissiveness is like playing Russian roulette.

It is an interesting commentary on the times when one who carefully weighs his words might be called a "bore" by the social set, while the one who can maintain a steady babble of nothings is considered a good conversationalist. This, even though what he articulates may be a senseless collection of clichés and banalities colored with a totally negative tone.

If everyone spoke only when he had something important to say, and then only if he could say it in a creative and constructive way, it might suddenly become a silent world. Coffee breaks would become times of solitude, and the cocktail party would lose its reason for being. A tourist, spending the night in a small New England village, joined some men sitting around the general store. He tried several times to start a conversation, without success. Finally he asked, "Is there a law against talking in this town?" One man said, "Nope, no law against it ... but there is an understanding that no one's to speak unless he can improve upon the silence!"

Perhaps this is a little exaggerated, but it does point to the importance of control. We are verbal creatures, and things often need to be said. However, the person has a choice in what he says, and a responsibility to say it in ways that are positive. You are a child of God, which means you are a creature of the great I AM. But "death and life are in the power of the tongue" (Prov. 18:21). Your I AM power can lead you to greatness, or it can bind you in mediocrity. Positive speech will lead to power and achievement, while negative words about yourself and others will be like driving your car with the brakes on.

Paul voiced a great Truth when he said that your life can be changed by altering your thoughts. If you would like to change ... really change ... the best place to start is to brush up on your speech. Eliminate the negative clichés, the tendency toward self-effacement, the sharing of pessimistic proclamations. It may not make for good conversation, but it will surely lead to physical and financial conservation.

Overheard in a typical social gathering: "Oh, I feel simply terrible today. They say there is a bad virus going around, and I suppose I am coming down with it!" "I feel pretty horrible myself. It's the miserable job I am stuck with. You wouldn't believe the office politics. It will be the death of me yet!" And on and on ad nauseam.

Of course, we should be realistic about ourselves and life in general. There is little to be gained if we regularly sweep everything under the rug and refuse to face up to obvious problems that should be met. However, this is an important criterion in all verbal exchanges: *Let something good be said!* Remember the darkness is only dealt with positively if we bring a light. Even if criticism or correction may be called for, it can be done in a positive and loving manner. No matter what the problem, let something good be said! It is a very subtle and yet important aspect of meta-morality.

Jesus realized the importance of directing the name of the Lord in righteous ways. He constantly called himself *by* the name of the Lord, proclaiming the I AM of his nature. In John there are dozens of these "I AM" statements in which he claims the Truth of Being: *"I am the way, and the truth, and the life ... I am the resurrection and the life ... I am the good shepherd"* (Jn. 10, 11, 14). The authorities did not understand. In fact, few of the disciples did. He was simply declaring for himself that which all persons must ultimately declare for themselves. He did not set himself up as the great exception, pointing to his divinity, but rather as the great example of the I AM in its clearest focus, and thus revealing the divinity of man, of you and me. The authorities were enraged, and when he was on the verge of being stoned, he asked, for which good work did they want to stone him. They said: *For a good work we stone thee not; but for blasphemy; and because that thou, being a man, makest thyself God* (Jn. 10:33 ASV).

Eventually, Jesus was put out of the way as a dangerous heretic. His crime: breaking the commandments. And more particularly: taking the name of the Lord in vain. What the authorities did not see was that in breaking the commandments down to their basic essence, he was in fact fulfilling them; while in "keeping" them in crystallized form, they were in fact breaking them. He pointed out that while they kept the letter of the law, yet they "practiced the absence of God" by praying in vain repetitions, heaping up empty phrases, fasting to be seen of men, and preaching without practicing. They were concerned with morality and the letter; Jesus was concerned with metamorality and the Spirit.

Institutional religion, even today, puts chief emphasis on being good. But what is good? Obviously it is a judgment, and of course the judging is done by the clergy on the basis of scriptural law. But the shocking Truth is that this same scriptural law found Jesus lacking and crucified him. Someone once knelt down before him, saying, "*Good Master.*"

But he quickly demurred, saying, *"Why callest thou me good? None is good save ... God"* (Lk. 18:19 ASV).

Theological "goodness" means "keeping" the commandments, going to services, and fulfilling the various religious codes. Obviously, this leaves many unanswered questions, for occasionally a pillar of the religious congregation experiences a tragic turn of events, and people cry out, "How could such a good religious person suffer so?" It is as if they are suddenly questioning the "system." And well they should! For it is not the caprice of God but the action of divine law. In terms of morality, the person may have been a model of goodness. But in the larger frame of metamorality, we must question the level of consciousness and the quality of the spoken word. One may be "good" and still be extremely negative. One may engage in services of adoration of God and yet be filled with feelings of self-hate. There are no experiences unrelated to consciousness and the process of "bodying" it forth through the spoken word. The law is "As within, so without."

There is great need today for a renaissance in the practice of religion. Services of worship are devoted to "keeping" the commandments and the codes and creeds intact. The religious experience is a performance and the communicants mere spectators. But the communion of oneness is rarely present. It is *two-ness* with the person worshiping God. The experience often leads to feelings of self-abasement (miserable sinners).

Perhaps we need a new kind of service with the descriptive term "an experience of creative worth-ship." The goal would be to heighten the consciousness of the person, to change his self-limiting attitudes to those that are more positive and loving. The liturgy would be devoted to a joyous celebration of the self as the focus of an infinite idea. The person should go forward with a new feeling of self-worth, a new commitment toward the process of calling himself by the name of the Lord, and keeping the high watch of positive thinking and the creative use of I AM-directed words.

The most widespread breach of the essence of the third commandment is in the practice of prayer. Much that passes for prayer is "the practice of the *absence* of God." There is a tendency to pray *to* God as if He were an absentee landlord of the universe. The prayer may begin with "Dear Lord" and end with "Amen!" and still consist of an orgy of worry and self-pity in between. The invocation at a political convention might be just another political speech: "Thou knowest that this party is the salvation of the country!" But all this is to take the name of the Lord in vain, or to deal with the I AM falsely.

Jesus said: *"It is your Father's good pleasure to give you the kingdom"* (Lk. 12:32). How could we accept this concept and still assume that we must plead or intercede in order to receive help? Prayer should not be the attempt to turn on a light in God, but to turn on the light in us; and God is the light. It is not conditioning God to our needs, but conditioning our needs with the flow of God. It is not reaching for God, supplicating God, or in any way seeking help from God ... for God knows ... and God is. Prayer is a process of letting go of the human tendency to reach, resting quietly in the awareness that God is the answer even before we ask. Our need is to speak the word of Truth and let *"Thy kingdom come ... on earth as it is in heaven"* (Mt. 6:10).

This may be an audacious and shocking statement, but perhaps it is a shock to which we all need to expose ourselves: Praying to God about things is taking the name of the Lord in vain. God is present as a Presence, and as the Word which is *"very near you ... that you can do it"* (Deut. 30:14). Pray not *to* God, but *from* the consciousness of God. God is present as the reality of you. There is nowhere to go, no one to reach for, only a Presence to experience and to feel at one with. The need is to be still and know *that* I AM.

In the Old Testament the "name of the Lord" is Jehovah, Yahweh, or, in the Hebrew, YHWH. This word is an acronym of four Hebrew letters: YOD, HE, WAW and HE. It is said that the whole Hebrew alphabet is invested with the character of "YOD."

The other letters are a combination of this initial form. YOD is the symbol of "first principle."

The YOD is suggested by the sound of indrawing your breath. Form the word on the lips and voice it as you inhale. Spirit means breath. *There is a spirit in man: and the inspiration of the Almighty giveth them understanding* (Job 32:8 ASV). A feeling of support and of guidance and light comes through the divine flow that can symbolically be experienced when you voice the YOD while inhaling. It is an excellent symbol for instant prayer: the quick inhalation of the breath. In any time of crisis, before you can even formulate any kind of prayer thought, just draw in your breath while voicing YOD. It can suggest a sense of oneness and protection.

Emerson says: *Man is an inlet and may become an outlet to all there is in God.* It is something you can practice ... with great effect. Voice the word *God* on the in-breath, and then let it body-forth on the exhalation by whispering, "I am." "God" (inhale) and "I am" (exhale). The process involved is significant: First, you symbolically return to the beginning, oneness, wholeness, being. Then you call yourself by the name of the Lord by voicing the I AM.

Prayer power suddenly becomes apparent when you realize that you can couple this I AM energy with anything you desire: *I am now being guided in right and wise ways; I am one with the flow of radiant healing life, and my body is renewed and made whole; I am prosperous and successful in everything I undertake.*

It is important to remember that these affirmations are not magic formulas that dramatically make something happen. The words have power only when they are imbued with power, and that power flows forth from within. Jesus said: *When thou prayest, enter into thy closet* ... (Mt. 6:6 ASV), which is returning to the ground of being. It is turning from illness to allness, from weakness to strength, from insufficiency to all-sufficiency, from indecisiveness to guiding light.

Remember, too, that Jesus assured us that it is God's will to unfold His allness in us. No need for "vain repetitions" or pleading: Just say yes to the flow of life. This is what the I AM statement implies. It is the commitment of receptivity to divine "good pleasure."

To pray amiss is to take the name of the Lord in vain. Instead of praying *for* life or intelligence or love or substance, remember that you *are* God becoming life in you, becoming intelligence in you, becoming love in you. So your prayer becomes an affirmation in the name of the Lord: I AM life, I AM intelligence, I AM love, I AM substance.

The great thing about it all is that the I AM of you, your God self, is ever seeking to project itself into visibility *as* you. It is the very source of your desires at their highest level. What you want to be, you *can* be, for the desire is the intuitive awareness of your I AM. Thus you can affirm for yourself: I can be what I want to be, if I know that I AM.

Resolve to speak only words that you want to see manifest in your life; for by your words you are directing the creative power of Infinite Mind into positive or negative channels. Make a commitment to break through the third commandment and to call yourself *by* the name of the Lord in the right and wise and consistent use of I AM.

The
FOURTH
Commandment

*Remember the sabbath day, to keep it holy.
Six days you shall labor, and do all your
work; but the seventh day is a sabbath to
the Lord your God; in it you shall not do
any work ... for in six days the Lord made
heaven and earth, the sea, and all that is in
them, and rested the seventh day; therefore
the Lord blessed the sabbath day and hallowed it* (Ex. 20:8-11).

Without a doubt this commandment has done more for the observance of religion in Judaism and Christianity than any other. For it appears to establish unequivocally the special time for religious study and worship. Originally, it was set down arbitrarily with a multitude of prohibitions and restrictions and with the maximum penalty of death.

To get the full impact of the early practice of the Mosaic Law, read the story (Num. 15:32) of the man found gathering sticks on the Sabbath. There is no mention of why he was gathering sticks, but one can assume that it was a matter of a father gathering firewood to keep his family warm. But the commandments must be kept at all costs! So the culprit was brought before the elders, who condemned him to death by stoning. *And all the congregation ... stoned him with stones, and he died ... as the Lord commanded.* An interesting commentary on the prevailing God-concept! And on the fanatically rigid adherence to the Ten Commandments.

There is much confusion about the fourth commandment. What is the Sabbath day? And how does one keep it holy? You might say, "Everyone knows that the Sabbath day is Sunday." That is not correct. The Jews keep their Sabbath on Saturday, beginning with sundown on Friday. Among Christians, the Seventh-Day Adventists observe their Sabbath on Saturday. And, from a purely scriptural point of view, they are probably correct. Saturday is the seventh day of the week, which Genesis says is the Sabbath day that the Lord blessed and hallowed.

Sunday was probably redesignated as the Sabbath day by Christian theologians who thought it more fitting to honor the "first day of the week" when Jesus was resurrected from the dead. Actually, the Sunday Sabbath was not practiced widely until it was developed by the Scots and the Puritans, who became as emotional about it as the followers of Moses were about the "seventh day."

The religious traditions in America have evolved from many influences of our Puritan forebears. Thus the Sabbath day has become an institution with punishment for its breach, tailored slightly to meet our more civilized standards. People are no longer stoned, but it has been made a sin not to go to mass or to church. People have been conditioned to the churchgoing habit, chiefly out of fear of not going.

And, as Bliss Carman sings, "They're praising God on Sunday. They'll be all right on Monday. It's just a little habit they've acquired."

As part of the cultural and moralistic veneer of our modern society, it is important to be seen going to services on the Sabbath. It has become the badge of conventional respectability. At times it has been considered good politics to give high visibility to worship services in the White House.

The Puritan influence has also been responsible for "blue laws" and Sunday closing ordinances that prohibit some or all commerce in cities across the land. The courts have sometimes rendered opinions that certain items could be sold while other items are banned. In other words, one could pick up stones but not sticks on the Sabbath! A recent Supreme Court decision seems to have opened the way for the elimination of all Sunday restrictions. And there are those who are crying out that this is breaking the commandments. And it is true. For the decision may go a long way toward breaking the fourth commandment, reducing it to the basic essence, which is good.

One of the strange quirks of the Christian Sabbath is the hour of worship, eleven o'clock on Sunday morning. Has it ever occurred to you to question that time? Why eleven? Why not ten? Or twelve? Or even three in the afternoon? It might be startling to those who think of the eleven o'clock time as "God's hour" to find that it was set to accommodate farm people, for it is *halfway between milking times.* One may rightly wonder whether some of the rigid Mosaic codes may have such simple explanations.

There is much concern over what is called the "Secular Society." Preachers like to attribute this erosion of spiritual and moral values in the marketplace to the work of the devil. Without a doubt there is much that is immoral, and many who are amoral, in the world "out there." But it could be that at least part of the cause is in *Sabbatarianism,* a big word that means "worship of the Sabbath."

It is institutional religion that created the divisions of sacred and secular, and of holy days and week-days. The church is usually a place set apart, con-ducted by a clergy, who are a class set apart, on the Sabbath, which is a day set apart. There is a tendency to go through the performance on Sunday, and then to put it all back into the six-day closet of unconcern.

There is a great cry for a return to religion and for teaching basic morality and the keeping of the Ten Commandments. However, it may be that the greater need is for the teaching of metamorality and the breaking of the commandments, reducing the Mosaic law to its underlying spiritual Truth. One good place to begin is with the fourth commandment and its crystallized emphasis on keeping the Sabbath.

The key to the fourth commandment is in the Hebrew root word *shabbâth*, which means rest, inter-mission, desist from exertion. The emphasis is on the rhythmic flow of the universe: work *and* rest, out-pouring *and* infilling. Even as a piano teacher may use a metronome to help a child to develop a sense of rhythm, the fourth commandment, dealing with the literal Sabbath day, was intended to help the Israelites to put stress on resting for health, and on times of prayer and meditation for *re*creation.

However, the Sabbath practice in contemporary times should be adapted to the cultural facts of life. To become a slave to the Sabbath for its own sake is like being tied to a metronome. Jesus was once criticized for doing healing work on the Sabbath and for permitting his disciples to gather food. This was still a very serious infraction of the law even in that latter day. But Jesus saw the Sabbath in a more spiritual light. In one fell swoop he broke the fourth commandment down to its basic idea, as he said, "The Sabbath was made for man, not man for the Sabbath." Thus did he seek to promote the idea of the Sabbath on the level of consciousness, and not just as a set time or day of the week.

It is interesting that the fourth commandment emphasized prohibition of all kinds of work by all classes of workers. Undoubtedly, this has given rise to the modern day "rights of workers." But what about mothers and homemakers? In all times of history, while the men were caught up in a meticulous observance of the many religious practices, mother was still cooking and cleaning and caring for the family. Good reason for freedom movements for women, and for "breaking" and not just keeping the commandments.

In the Genesis story of creation, on the seventh day God rested. It seemed logical to assume that man, too, should rest on every seventh day. However, modern Bible scholarship and the facts of geological life have insisted that the creation story does not deal with time, but with stages of unfoldment. The seven steps of the creation outline a process that is just as relevant to building a house as creating a world. From a more metaphysical perspective, the seventh day of creation implies, "When you have put your mind, heart and hands to a project, then let go and let God breathe life into it that it may become a living form."

The native Hawaiians have an unusual word for visitors to the islands: *haolis*. It seems that when the Christian missionaries first arrived, they set about to convert the natives from their pagan ways. They set up little chapels in which the people should worship God. Being a peace-loving people, the natives were easily led into the new discipline. But they found one thing quite strange. Whereas in their Kahuna practice they always followed their times of worship of the gods with a period of silence "to breathe life into their devotions," the Christians simply rattled off their prayers and got up and walked out. So the natives called the Christians, and later all visitors to the islands, *haolis*. The word means without breath.

This is the spirit of the fourth commandment. *"Remember the sabbath day, to keep it holy."* Take time to let Spirit breathe life into your whole being, to pause and become centered in the divine flow of life, love and substance. The word *holy* means whole. There is a wholeness within you always. Wherever Spirit is at all the whole of Spirit must be. And, because Spirit is omnipresent, the whole of Spirit must be present in its entirety at every point in space at the same time. The Sabbath day is the time, any time, when you remember the allness of God that is present right where you are as the fullness of all that you are and all that you need or desire.

To keep the Sabbath holy is to do your work, whatever and wherever it may be, in the awareness of the divine flow of power, intelligence and creativity. Do what you do with enthusiasm and vigor, and then, synchronizing with the rhythm of the universe, take time occasionally to pause, let go, and enter the inner chamber and shut the door.

In every city there may be seen marvelously committed people who get up a little earlier every morning to attend a mass or service on their way to work. Others may run off to a chapel for a time of prayer or meditation during their lunch hour. This, in itself, is to break through the surface meaning of the fourth commandment and its one-day-a-week Sabbath. However, a little less conspicuous but no less committed are the thousands of people who practice some form of meditation right where they happen to be, at home or at work. Charles Fillmore pointed to the ultimate in Sabbath-keeping when he said that within every person there is a church service going on all the time, and one needs only to enter in and experience it.

As I have repeatedly stressed, the commandments were created by Moses as important guidelines for primitive people. Even as a parent builds a fence around the yard to restrain the wandering toddler, and then progressively eliminates it as the child matures and understands the reasons for self-discipline ... so Moses created the Decalogue of "Thou shalt nots," containing positive aids to self-realization that are fully understood only as they are progressively broken out of their crystallized shells.

The Sunday Sabbath observance is important as a metronome of balance. We should not take it lightly, for until we get a sense of rhythm of life, we need its continued reminder to take time to infill. But it is not enough simply to have Sunday away from work. The worker may demand Sunday off, and then get into projects equally as draining, and even "moonlight" on another job. Americans typically have such frantic weekends of busyness that they may look forward to going back to work on Monday to rest up. In the process it may be that the Sunday holy day has become a hollow day.

One meaning of Sabbath is "period of rest." How many persons engage in true resting on the Sabbath? Or even think of rest? Most persons who think of themselves as very religious give Sunday rest little thought. They may attend worship services some-where, and then spend the remainder of the day at golf or a ballgame or weeding the garden or driving to the beach or the mountains. Rest is the furthest thing from the mind or experience of most persons on weekends.

Does this imply that one should just sit and twiddle his thumbs hour after hour on Sunday? Of course not. Boredom will get us nowhere. I simply want to point out how unrealistic and even hypocritical our Sunday Sabbath attitudes have become. The true Sabbath is not just a day, and does not involve just "going to services." These things are excellent disciplines, and all those whose early training included them are better for it as adults. But keeping the Sabbath holy is more a matter of creating new patterns of living in which the spiritual "pause that refreshes" is equally as important as the work to achieve.

A highly successful businessman has a prayer time in his office every morning at ten o'clock. This has been a morning ritual with him for more than 25 years. His secretary takes no calls and all business must wait while he has his 10-minute Sabbath. Yet the man never goes to church and regularly plays golf on Sunday. His religious friends call him a sinner and pray for his salvation. Actually, the man's church is an inner experience that he faithfully observes every day. Is not this more spiritually infilling than a once-a-week show of going to services?

This is not to denigrate the church or to criticize frequent Sunday attendance. The world needs what the churches can give, and every person may be immeasurably blessed by being a part of that giving. However, churches could be much more effective and Sunday attendance would be much greater if the emphasis were more on teaching than on preaching, on helping people to find their spiritual center within rather than on demanding loyalty to a place of stone and stained glass. There is growing awareness today, even among churchmen, that the declining influence of the church is in large measure due to *ecclesiolatry*— another big word meaning "worship of the church."

Henry Drummond, the Scottish preacher, angered many of his confreres in the ministry when he said that the main purpose of the Church was to help people to get along without it. He was not espousing the breakup of the Church but rather the breaking down of its creeds into a practical way of life. He was saying that the Church should see itself like a school or a college, whose role is to make the student a self-reliant person and to make itself progressively unnecessary. He felt that a good Christian was not just a faithful Sunday communicant, but one who experienced his communion with God often, wherever he might be, by entering the quiet sanctuary of the soul.

To remember the Sabbath day is to periodically check up on yourself to determine if you are moving, thinking, working, loving and living in the flow of universal rhythm. You might sit on the beach and reflect on the ebb and flow of the tide, or watch the rising and setting of the sun. Then, become aware of your body and feel the same balancing rhythms at work: the beat of your heart, the constancy of the diastole and systole. Did you know that there is a contraction and dilation of the heart 75 times a minute, week after week, month after month, and year after year as long as you live? How can this organ work so hard and for so long? By frequent rest and renewal. You see, the heart is not constantly at work. Following every contraction there is a vital period of relaxation. Studies have revealed that out of every 24 hours the heart is still for a total of 15 hours. Isn't that amazing? It is this rest schedule that enables the heart to go without stopping for scores of years. The heart, thus, has its constant Sabbath.

Have you ever noticed that, on finishing a job or a difficult problem, there is a tendency to heave a sigh? It is a symbol of relief and release from tension. This is a kind of Sabbath. And beyond the sigh comes an inbreathing that could symbolize an inflow of the Spirit. Experience this right now: Heave a sigh ... and then draw in a long breath. Let the sigh indicate the completion of the creation, the Sabbath rest, and then think of the long inhalation as the *inspiration of the Almighty* [that] *giveth them understanding* (Job 32:8 ASV). Remember to make this identification with the sigh that invariably follows any task. It is but one small step beyond this to the disciplined practice of the presence of God all through your day.

To keep the Sabbath means to discipline yourself to regular periods of prayer or meditation. To keep the Sabbath holy means to do all that you do in the awareness of inner power, and thus to have frequent silent parentheses to remember your oneness with the divine flow.

Inherent in the Sabbath process is the experience of *creative resting*. It is a kind of relaxation that involves more than simply physical inaction. It is plugging in to the divine action that makes the physical possible and vital. It is not just a matter of sleeping. For one may sleep without creatively resting, and one can rest well without sleeping. This is an important thing to remember when, for instance, you fall asleep during a meditation. Do not feel guilty about it, for you probably needed the sleep. But later, you can and should resume the practice of creative resting.

You may say, "But why should I rest when I am not tired?" Actually, many persons are tied up in bundles of mental and physical tension even without knowing it. Some persons may not have truly relaxed for years. In this frustration of the divine flow it is extremely difficult not only to fulfill your capacity for happiness and success, but to get a sense of oneness.

The old hymn sings, "Take time to be holy." Take time to become established in the consciousness of wholeness, oneness with the divine flow. The benefits are great. You will increase your ability to make decisions and to unfold creative ideas. You will be "in the world but not of it." You will easily rise above the challenges of human relations. And you will regularly experience the most effective beauty treatment. It will iron out harsh lines from the face and smooth away the bags under the eyes. It will improve your disposition and your health. In the marketplace of life peace may seem elusive and even unattainable, but it comes easily to the mind that is disciplined to creative resting.

By all means keep the fourth commandment. Go to church on Sunday when and if you can. But do not delude yourself by thinking that your Sabbath obligation ends at twelve noon on Sunday. Let it be a time of practice of the principle and process of oneness which is integral to every moment and every experience of your life. You are a spiritual being, with the responsibility to unfold your "imprisoned splendor" all along life's way. Make the commitment to walk that way in holiness, in wholeness.

When you have broken the fourth commandment out of its traditional shell, you will be free forever from the binding concept that the creative flow of God comes only on a special day or in a special place. You will know that the Presence is always present, wherever you may be. And then the true essence of the commandment will be made real: Get in tune with life's universal rhythm through regular periods of creative resting, and, as in Genesis, God *breathed into his nostrils the breath of life; and man became a living being* (Gen. 2:7). Not just in a once-and-for-all experience, but in a constant rhythmic process, and of course, calling for commitment and daily practice.

The
FIFTH
Commandment

Honor your father and your mother, that your days may be long in the land which the Lord your God gives you (Ex. 20:12).

This commandment is a sentimental favorite. How good it is to see aged parents cared for and respected by their families. Every culture that has long survived has included in its religious or philosophic creeds some kind of teaching similar to the fifth commandment. Among the Jews it was a sacred duty, bound by law. In fact, in Exodus 21:17, it is clearly stated that one who curses his parents is to be put to death.

Against this backdrop Jesus' revolutionary concept is the more startling. For He said: *"Call no man your father on earth, for you have one Father, who is in heaven"* (Mt. 23:9). And if that is not shocking enough, he said *"If any one comes to me and does not hate his own father and mother and wife and children and brothers and sisters ... he cannot be my disciple"* (Lk. 14:26). No wonder Jesus was considered a dangerous rebel. It was rank heresy!

And yet Jesus said that he was not trying to destroy the law, but to fulfill it. As discussed in "The Second Commandment," it is not likely that he was suggesting abandonment of parents, for we have the example of his own tenderness toward his mother. George Lamsa, leading scholar in the Aramaic origins of the New Testament, says that the word *hate* as used here is a mistranslation, and that it should be *put aside.* Thus, Jesus does not destroy the spirit of the fifth commandment. He breaks it down to its basic essence to reveal new and far-reaching implications.

All the commandments evolve out of the basic "One." The Lord God is One! Every person lives in the One and is of the One. When we place too much emphasis on the role of parents, we make graven images of them. The "god-father syndrome," which exists in most family relationships in a greater or lesser degree, is too often stifling of individuality and personal development. One may be born into a family where the chief training is based on family unity, respect for elders, attachment to brothers and sisters, and "blood is thicker than water." He may be so conditioned to this system that he matures and lives out his whole life never daring to think that his own unfoldment as a person has any place in the scheme of things. Or if he does secretly hunger for knowledge of his divine identity, he may be filled with pangs of guilt.

Jesus was saying that if you are so attached to your parents or to your own offspring that you let them stand in the way of your soul unfoldment, then you are not worthy of the creative flow. Honor your mother and father and your whole family relationship by freeing each person to his own experience, and accept that freedom for yourself.

The word *honor* may become a cliché. To honor your parents in a perfunctory manner may create a façade that covers many less-than-honorable feelings. Thus *honor* is an anemic word, similar to the word *tolerance*. Tolerance of people has been called a Christian duty. It implies a grin-and-bear-it kind of cordiality, even if there are strong dislikes. So the traditional approach to religion is "Keep the commandments." They are your parents so you must honor them, send them cards for birthdays and anniversaries, and occasionally "pay the old folks a visit."

Consider the paradox of Mother's Day. Even if there may be little communication through the year, or if there are smoldering feelings of resentment for the psychological scars we are carrying, which we are certain are the result of parental mistreatment in the early years ... despite all this, on this one day we send the card and special gift, place the long-distance phone call, or pay the visit. One day honoring and praising and feting this "mother o' mine." And then back to 364 days of indifference and neglect. Why not turn it all around? Why not have an annual "hate your mother day"? On this one day write a letter or make a phone call and get all the frustrated feelings out in the open. And then spend the remaining days of the year treating this person humanely and respectfully. We are joking; but not entirely so. What we are saying is that if you are going to keep the fifth commandment, then keep it sincerely and not just by means of an occasional greeting card.

The word *honor* comes from the Hebrew root word *kâbad*, which literally means "burdensome." The commandment really says, "Accept the burden of your father and mother." But this needs to be broken down further, for if you deal with your parents in this consciousness, there may be much hidden frustration and bitterness. This might give rise to feelings of guilt on the part of the offspring, and also to unreasonable demands on the part of the parents: "I am your mother. You owe me respect and support. I brought you into the world, and don't you ever forget it!"

"Call no man your father on earth, for you have one Father." "You are a spiritual being, and the divine tie always transcends the blood tie. You will never be

able to fit into any human relationship, whether father, mother, sister or brother, until you can see yourself as first, last, and always a child of God, centered in your own divine flow. The "burden" is that you are heavy with child: the Christ of your being, the whole creature that you are created ultimately to become. Within you is the unborn possibility of limitless experience, and yours is the privilege and responsibility of giving birth to it.

The fifth commandment, then, tells us to respect ourselves, accept the burden of the Christ child within, and let it unfold our experience, that God, the true father-mother parenting process within us, may do its nurturing work. And we have a responsibility, not just the freedom, to let nothing stand in the way of this unfoldment. As Meister Eckhart might put it, "No matter what the relationship, your first loyalty must be to the divine flow within ... and to let God *be* God in you."

In his *Cocktail Party*, T. S. Eliot characterizes the plight of so many homes that are established by two people who have no sense of the divine flow:

> *They do not repine;*
> *Are contented with the morning that separates*
> *And with the evening that brings together*
> *For casual talks before the fire*
> *Two people who know they do not understand*
>   *each other,*

Breeding children whom they do not under-
stand
And who will never understand them.

It is a great mistake to teach children to respect their parents at all costs. "After all, he is your father." For if the child is forced to respect someone who is not worthy of respect, he will eventually lose respect for himself. The child must be led to accept the "burden" of his own divine potential. If he accepts and respects himself as an integral part of the divine flow, he will naturally have love and understanding for his parents. But it will be a mature love based on the honest recognition of failings and the willingness to understand how they have come about.

Out of a sense of personal insecurity parents often hunger for a glorified parental role. Then they may seek a sense of personal significance in being the center of attention and the seat of authority. A young mother may talk of "making a baby," which can lead to possessiveness with the children ... and guilt and frustration if the child does not turn out to be whole physically, or even morally. All prospective parents should read Kahlil Gibran's excellent treatise "On Children" in his classic book, *The Prophet*. He says: *Your children are not your children. They are the sons and daughters of life's longing for itself. They come through you but not from you, and though they are with you yet they belong not to you.*

Emerson touches on a point of balance when he says that one should not be too much a parent. Not that the child should grow up without direction or discipline, but that the discipline should encourage him to become who he is, to develop in the way that is more natural to his uniqueness. All too often the proud parent is not content to have the child grow up in conformity with his natural bent, so he projects his own desire for glory into the child.

Instead of keeping the fifth commandment in its static sentimental form, we need to break it down to the idea of honoring the father-mother principle within every person, and the importance of respecting the unfolding process of divine sonship. It becomes a commandment that is more applicable to the fathers and mothers than to their offspring. Instead of insisting on respect for his children, the parent will be more concerned that the child develops a healthy respect for himself. The parent will not demand special homage because the child happens to be born of his seed, or because he is supported. Why should the parent demand gratitude from his children because he is caring for them in the way that all living creatures do for their offspring? If they respect him, he should want that respect for human reasons, not just filial. He should be more concerned about respecting their individuality, honoring their privacy, and encouraging their intellectual and spiritual growth.

A good parent should be mature enough so that his first concern should not be that his children like him, but that they like what God intends them to be as persons. And certainly, if the children recognize and appreciate this attitude on the part of their parents, the parents can feel secure that the children will respect and love them as persons and honor them as parents.

Often, in the face of some delinquency or depravity among young people, there will be a great call for "moral values," and for old-fashioned virtues of respect for elders. It is disturbing to many persons to note how the traditional values of honor and respect for parents and elders are being rejected by the younger generation. The fifth commandment is being questioned ... and broken. However, the need is not for morality, but for metamorality, not just for the façade of respect of elders by the young, but for a more universal insight into the divine parenting process within all persons. When there is a greater respect for spiritual law, a greater awareness that all persons are one with the One, and one in the One, then there will be a universal respect for self and for the divine flow in the self. Parents will respect themselves and their children, and children will respect themselves and their parents. Parents, as wise stewards, will seek to make themselves progressively unnecessary. And the young will seek to get and keep in their own creative flow. In this way they will come to a behavior that is acceptable not by conforming to values that are set for them, but rather by being transformed by the renewal of their minds.

This leads to another more subtle meaning of the fifth commandment. It involves the acceptance of personal responsibility for your life. What you think and say and do today will have a profound influence on what you will one day become. In the same sense, we could trace many influences in years past that have molded and shaped your growth and unfoldment to where you are today. A speaker once addressed a high school assembly on the subject "Be Good to Your Old Man!" The students were expecting some trite Sunday school moralizing. Instead, the talk turned out to be something entirely different, an insight that made a lifelong impression on those youthful listeners. What the man said was, "Be careful what patterns you form today in thought and act, for it will have much to do with the person you will become in later years." The "old man" is the person who will evolve out of the person you now are. The child is the parent of the adult.

You may say, "You have touched on my problem, for how can I honor my father and mother when my life has been ruined by the rejection and mistreatment I had as a child?" It is true that these early relationships, the absence of affection, the critical abuse, and the hostility between your parents had a strong formative influence on your unfoldment. However, even if your parents have long since passed on, there is much that you can do today. You can love them and forgive them.

"They do not deserve my love!" you may say. But that is not the point. Don't you deserve it? You need to be in the flow of love constantly. This is why Jesus says; *"Love your enemies ... that you may be sons of your Father"* (Mt. 5:44). In other words, wherever there is enmity or unforgiveness, love, so that you can get yourself in tune with the creative process of God. For the thoughts you entertain today, even if they pertain to something that happened long ago, are, in fact, setting up causes for that which will happen tomorrow and tomorrow.

But how, you may object, can you be held accountable for things your parents did to you in your childhood? You were too young to take charge of your own mind and emotions. True, but they were *your* mind and *your* emotions. And you were hurt because you were hurt-able. However, the resulting state of your mind that has harassed you through the years has not been all bad. Many successes and achievements have been the result of your attempt to overcompensate for your insecurity or inadequacy.

You have been led to explore paths of growth that you might not otherwise have experienced. And, even more, it is likely that something in your own soul attracted your parents and the very kind of treatment to which you were subjected.

Now, that is all past. You cannot change it. But you can take charge of your life today and control what all these things do to you in your present experience. First of all, you must forgive all those who you feel have hurt you, neglected you, or in any way frustrated your good. More, you must forgive yourself, that little child who is the parent of the one you have become today. It has all come to pass ... let it go. Open the way now for all things to work together for good, even if the "good" is the painful challenges that have forced you to grow. Growth is what life is about. Be grateful.

You may say, "What about all those wasted years of bitterness, and loneliness?" There is no way you can have them back to live over. But you can be free from their burden. The prophet Joel said: *"I will restore to you the years which the swarming locust has eaten"* (Joel 2:25). The word *restore* comes from the Hebrew word *buwsh*, which literally means to heal, to make new. When you honor or accept the burden of your parents, you are set free from the limitations of the past. You are free from the sense of "wasted years." Because they are significant years of growth, you are free from resentment, free to take the best and leave the rest, free to walk on.

One young man, whose relationships with his mother through all the formative years of his life had been extremely negative, has come to a very self-honest realization. Though he had been "pounded on" for years with the psychological blows of criticism and belittlement amid tantrums of crying and screaming, he has survived and matured. He has admitted to himself that his ambition and creative drive have been the constant attempt to prove that he is not as unworthy as his mother's treatment had made him feel. So today he reflects, "What my mother did to me has had a profound influence on what I have done to and for myself. And, quite frankly, I like what I have become, so I am truly grateful to my mother." Today, he has his own family, and maturity has brought understanding. He now can honestly keep the fifth commandment.

Another side of this coin of taking responsibility for your life is the awareness that those things that you establish in consciousness today are the patterns that will unfold themselves in the years to come. To "honor your father and your mother" also means to accept the burden of your present state of consciousness that is the parent of what you will become in the years ahead.

Keep your thoughts wholly on God, on Truth, on those things that you want to see manifest in your life. When you think or speak or act in negative ways, you are mortgaging your future. Your present attitudes and feelings, no matter that you may blame them on what someone else is doing or saying about you, are creating the conditions that make the results inevitable. Choose your moods, choose your thoughts, choose to keep yourself in perfect peace. This is to honor your father and mother.

One of the most limiting ways that we lay traps for ourselves, or mortgage our future, is in making or taking vows. If you impetuously proclaim, "I will never speak to him again as long as I live," you are limiting your future experience to your present low state of consciousness. Usually one comes to regret such a vow. Either you will break it with a sense of weakness of character or hold to it stoically, feeling trapped by a regrettable decision.

An alcoholic may vow never to take another drink. How easily that vow is broken, reducing his already low self-esteem. How much better to take the vow for one day only, to live and work in "day-tight compartments." At the end of the day he can have the satisfaction of accomplishment, and then can progress for another day. Even if he fails, he can pick himself up and plunge into the promise of the new day to come.

Many churches require vows to keep certain tenets of the faith, such as the Ten Commandments. Actually, if a person works at his religion as a practice of living principles, he will grow in understanding of himself and of life. He cannot go on holding the same views as the years pass. How much better for the sincere student of any spiritual philosophy to commit himself to the practice of Truth that is "open-ended" in scope. He must keep his mind open and his heart receptive to the constancy of change. This is to honor the "father-mother principle" that forever works within him, and to be good to the "old man," the unfolding process of what he will eventually become.

In the Leviticus version of the Ten Commandments, the fifth commandment adds the phrase "that it may go well with you." Honor and respect the process at work in the parenting principle of the mind, and it will go well with you, "your days will be long in the land which the Lord your God gives you." It is the assurance of abundance that follows in the wake of the harmonious application of divine law. Jesus summed it up when he said: *"Seek first his kingdom and his righteousness, and all these things shall be yours as well"* (Mt. 6:33).

The
SIXTH
Commandment

You shall not kill (Ex. 20:13).

In any discussion of the problems of the world or of our society, sooner or later someone will say smugly, "Well, if people would just obey the Ten Commandments ..." It is the great cliché! For who knows them, or really understands their implications in modern times?

A good illustration of the hypocrisy of the "live by the Ten Commandments" platitude is the sixth commandment: *"You shall not kill."* Four words, plain and simple, no qualifications. Does the frenetic advocate of the Decalogue keep this commandment and accept its implications unequivocally? No killing at all ... no destruction of life of any kind ... no eating meat ... no killing insects ... no killing in self-defense ... no capital punishment ... no war.

Suddenly our "back to the Ten Commandments" man runs for cover. Then begins his array of rationalizations: "But we must eat meat to get sufficient protein ... and actually Jesus ate meat. We have a right to kill in self-defense. Society has a right to kill offenders. A nation has a right to kill enemies in war." Of course he deplores war (and it is interesting that generals are among the greatest deplorers), but he has no doubt that God is on the side of the "just nation."

Where does all this leave the commandment, "You shall not kill"? We are left with the inescapable conclusion that no one really takes it literally. Practically everyone, if pressed on the issue, would insist that under certain circumstances it is right and proper to kill. While there are those who flout the commandments, we must face up to the fact that even those who "keep" them do not really believe them or practice them in their lives.

For instance, "You shall not kill" has been an enigma to the whole world of Christianity, Islam and Judaism for thousands of years. Certainly, the most ferocious and brutal of wars have been religious wars under these banners. The Christians have even glorified warfare by singing "Onward, Christian soldiers, marching as to war."

Yes, it would be a wonderful world if people just followed the Ten Commandments! But the problem is not that we make an earnest effort to follow them and fail, but that when it comes right down to specifics, such as "You shall not kill," we simply interpret them as we want. And we turn away from the issue conveniently, offering the rationalistic concept of Ecclesiastes 3:3: *A time to kill, and a time to heal; a time to break down, and a time to build up.*

In retrospect, and in the hindsight that has led to the conclusion that the last war was futile, many persons are now wondering how we could have been so resistant to war resisters and to movements promoting nonviolence ... and how we could have so blindly covered our transparent abandonment of the sixth commandment with the cry of patriotism. There are many lessons to be learned from these national and personal experiences. Are we willing to look honestly at them and learn from them?

It is interesting how many arguments are set forth against such things as gun control—even though guns are made to kill. If there is anything that symbolizes the willful breach of the letter of the sixth commandment, it is a gun. No matter that it is reserved for hunting or for self-defense, it is, and it was intended to be, a lethal weapon. Needless to say, the vast majority of murders are done, not by criminals after premeditation, but by average persons, even churchgoers who swear by the Ten Commandments. The killing is done on the spur of the moment, and a handy gun simply "spurs the moment."

Without a doubt the sixth commandment has been the basis for the myriad legal codes and moral restraints that have produced the cultural awareness we call "civilization." But we must admit that compliance with this emphatic command has been extremely selective.

Some persons, especially the most traditional religionists, may be shocked at my repeated suggestion that we need to learn, not how to keep the commandments, but how to "break" them. As I have pointed out, the concept is not at all original. Jesus was the great iconoclast, seeking to break down the commandments, codes and observances into a more relevant and practical form. For instance, he said: *"You have heard that it was said to the men of old, 'You shall not kill; and whoever kills shall be liable to judgment.' But I say to you that every one who is angry with his brother shall be liable to judgment; whoever insults his brother shall be liable to the council, and whoever says, 'You fool!' shall be liable to the hell of fire"* (Mt. 5:21, 22).

Instead of trying to narrow the sixth commandment into the strict ethical sense of who can be killed and who can kill, Jesus broadened the application into the whole area of destructive tendencies of mind. Jesus was like a wily prosecutor who allowed you no room to evade issues, no place to hide. There is no way, in his concept of "You shall not kill," for anyone to sit back and, clucking his tongue, say, "Yes, if *they* would just obey, we would have a good world!" With Jesus, it was never *them*, only you!

Jesus said, further: *"You have heard that it was said, 'An eye for an eye and a tooth for a tooth.' But I say to you, Do not resist one who is evil. But if any one strikes you on the right cheek, turn to him the other also"* (Mt. 5:38, 39). This deals with the basic human desire for revenge. Jesus' ideal was the power of transcendence. You may not be able to change the outer situation, but you can always rise above it by turning to a higher level of consciousness. We tell our children, "There is a 'little me' and a 'great me' in all of us." The "little me" reacts in anger and seeks revenge. The "great me" is always established in love and poise. Turn the other cheek. Turn from hostility to love.

There is a wise saying: "You may not be able to keep the birds from flying over your head, but you can keep them from building nests in your hair." Things may happen around you and even to you, but if they "get under your skin" it is because you have permitted them to happen within you.

Jesus also said: *"You have heard that it was said, 'You shall love your neighbor and hate your enemy.' But I say to you, Love your enemies and pray for those who perse-cute you, so that you may be sons of your Father"* (Mt. 5:43-45). To have an enemy is to have enmity. This is always the focus of the problem. Your feelings of enmity frustrate the flow of love. He said that you should love them and bless them so that you can re-establish your oneness with the divine flow.

In ancient Egypt there was a pharaoh who had this insight into love and nonresistance well ahead of his time. It was the time-honored custom of putting to death all captured soldiers. However, he would talk with them, forgive them, and release them. His critics were incensed and on the verge of rebellion. His response: 'What, do I not destroy my enemies when I love them?"

Divine law is inexorable in its function. It is supportive if we understand it and keep within its right action. However, because it is law and not caprice, there is a swift comeback in consciousness and experience if we resist it. It is vitally important that every person realize this basic function of the universe. If we are angry with someone, no matter what he may have done or how we may defend our "righteous indignation," we reap the effects in our minds, bodies and affairs ... and often swiftly.

This goes to the crux of all so-called justifiable murder, such as war or capital punishment. The principle is "The incident is external; the reaction is our own." We may seek retaliation or vengeance for what others have done. We may want to punish them. But how we deal with them is an activity of our consciousness. There is always a price to pay! *If any one slays with the sword, with the sword must he be slain!* (Rev. 13:10).

Whenever a criminal is executed on the gallows or in a gas chamber, some persons may feel very right about it, or at least think that it is a necessary deterrent to further crime. However, in the process of "killing by the sword," every member of the society that condones it is degraded, and there is a rip in the fabric of society as a whole. By the law of consciousness the "kill" state of mind will simply set into force a new wave of negative vibrations that create the environment in which more criminals and killers are spawned.

As long as societies wage war, no matter what the provocation or holy cause, those societies are projecting a negative energy causation that will continue to come back upon those same societies. As long as societies promote and use instruments of force and of killing, we are in the spirit of war and we will constantly draw to ourselves war situations. In debates on disarmament, there is usually a frantic cry, "We need weapons to defend ourselves!" A logical argument, but a logic that leads to the "eye for an eye" attitude that always justifies entrance into war. A new kind of transcendental logic is needed, a new application of metamorality. It is time to create new concepts of international law. Violence between individuals is a misdemeanor in most societies, but violence between nations is war with laws to regulate how it shall be conducted. It is like demanding "humane" means of employing capital punishment. Or setting down rules for stealing ... how much one may steal and at what time of the day or night.

If we can ban chemical and germ warfare, why should we not outlaw bombs and even guns? If we can establish international rules for the conduct of wars, we surely can agree on rules for the maintenance of peace. Of course, first we will have to take seriously the sixth commandment, to admit that killing, all killing, breaks universal law and sets up forces of causation that will inexorably bring more problems for humankind. When will we learn ... and begin to wage peace as relentlessly as we sometimes wage war?

The physical act of violence that leads to killing is really an attempt to destroy something that appears to be a threat to the person. We are vindictive to the killer, not because he had killing thoughts, but only that he did not control them. Actually, we condone killing thoughts in ourselves. One might say, "I could kill him for that!" Of course he would say, "But I really didn't mean it literally." And yet Jesus leaves no room for explanations. He says if you are angry at someone, you have already broken the "you shall not kill" commandment. In consciousness you have already put yourself at cross-purposes with the law.

How do we change the pattern? First, by getting a deeper awareness of the sixth commandment: *"You shall not kill."* It is a restraining wall that a wise society has used to keep people in line. It is like "No Smoking" and "Keep Off the Grass." But remember, as Moses set them forth, the commandments are not merely prohibitions, but statements of divine law that are phrased in the "you shall not" language for the spiritually immature. It is like telling a child, "Do not leave the yard." However, the commandments are not intended to say, "You had better be good or God will punish you!" Instead, they are saying, "Don't delude yourself. You cannot break the law ... simply because it *is* law. If you try to break it, you break yourself upon it."

The higher meaning of the sixth commandment is "You *cannot* kill." Your violent acts or thoughts relative to that which seems to threaten you is your attempt to destroy it. Actually, there is no way that you can destroy it, because the real problem is your mistaken belief. Jesus said that a man's enemies are those of his own household—in other words, the thoughts of his own mind. The only way you can destroy the enemy is through love—changing the level of your thinking. The true enemy is your enmity, which can be corrected only by you and in you.

The person who is always angry at the world is really angry within and at himself. Psychiatrists say that most people who do violent things are acting out of paranoia, and the problems and the supposed "enemies" are essentially the creation of their own imagination.

There are people who start lashing out at the world as soon as they get up in the morning ... and they keep the battle going all day long. First, they grumble about the weather, then they find fault with their wives, husbands, children or in-laws. On their way to work they push and shove on buses, subways and commuter trains ... or lean on their horns in the continuous traffic jams. In conversation they complain about the high cost of living, taxes, the stock market and last night's terrible television shows. During coffee breaks they collect in clans to gossip about Bill's ex-girlfriend or Hilda's new hair-do. Then at five o'clock there is a repeat of the scramble for seats and the fight for the right-of-way. And through it all there are many violent thoughts, such as, "That just kills me" and "I could kill him" ... and so very much of the kind of anger that Jesus said is breaking the sixth commandment.

It all comes from the delusive feeling that things "out there" can hurt you or take away that which is yours. This is your own paranoia, which may be quite subtle. The sixth commandment implies that nothing exterior to you can harm you or hinder you, except as you give it entrance into your mind. Here it becomes self-destructive and emotionally, physically and even financially frustrating. Remember, it is *your* mind, no matter that you are angry or bitter about something that happened to you. If it happens *in* you, it is due to your reaction.

No one can hurt your character, destroy your peace of mind, or make you angry. People and conditions can and often do provide you with many opportunities for inner turmoil and self-pity. But if you succumb to the temptation, it is because, either by habit or conscious choice, you have determined that this is the way you are going to meet it. You cannot do much about the things out there that we often go to war inwardly and outwardly over; but you can work on the thoughts you hold about them. You can get a greater consciousness of love and harmony. You can "agree with your adversary" because the only true adversary is the adverse reactions to people or conditions in your mind. The word *agree* comes from a root word that means to be "well-minded." When you become "well-minded" in the face of chaotic things, they will begin to dissolve.

Many persons waste their lives thinking how they are being hurt, held back, or damaged by others.

They feel that other people are standing in their way, and "how good it would be" if it were not for some person or organization or nation. As long as they think like this, they are standing in their own way. When we really catch the spirit and the Truth of "you cannot kill," we are free to be and do what we want.

The greatest lessons can often be learned from the lowliest expressions of life. Consider the lowly oyster. Grains of sand work themselves into its shell and irritate it. It tries to get rid of them. When it cannot do so, it settles down and produces one of the most beautiful things in the world. It turns its irritation into a pearl. When something is irritating you and causing a reaction of anger, just remember that it is totally impractical and uneconomical to indulge in the kind of killing thoughts that will eventually come back on you. Solve your irritation in a simple way: get busy pearling.

Realize that the reaction proves that there is something out of order in your consciousness. Bless the person who appears to have caused it for showing you where your weak point is. Then get to work agreeing with your adversary, knowing that the adversary is the adverse thoughts of your mind. Turn the other cheek to a manner that is well-minded. Get back in the flow ... with a right attitude toward yourself and life. Get busy pearling.

The
SEVENTH
Commandment

You shall not commit adultery (Ex. 20:14).

T his commandment is an interesting paradox. Moralistic religion that led to Puritanism and Victorianism gave rise to prudery so severe that the word *adultery* could not be used in polite company. The commandment was rarely if ever discussed, and then only in whispers. In the period in which many of us grew up, even the word *sex* was a naughty word.

How this has all changed in the past 30 years! Today there is more of a tendency to "tell it like it is," even if what *is* is not particularly uplifting. There are those who say that this indicates an increase in immorality in our day. However, it may mean only that there is a decrease in hypocrisy. People may not be any less moral today ... only more honest.

Turning from an attitude that has been irrational, prejudiced and blind, we have been helped by the work of Kinsey and Masters and Johnson and others to discover some aspects of human behavior that have long lurked in the shadows. Pious preachments about sin and immorality will serve little purpose other than to close the blinds again. Perhaps we need to face the fact that "keeping" the seventh commandment has failed miserably. Now we must break it down into its spiritual fundamentals. It is not morality that is required, but an understanding of meta-morality.

Words are an interesting study. For instance: *adult* and *adulterate* have nothing in common other than their sound. One person said, "Adultery is an adult playing around." It is a logical conclusion, but an erroneous one. The word *adult* is from the Latin past participle of *adolescere*, meaning to grow up. *Adulterate*, on the other hand, means to pollute, or to add something other. Our word *adultery* comes from the second word, not the first. One might logically assume, again in error, that even as infancy is the normal state for the infant, so adultery is the normal state for the adult.

From its Hebrew root, *adultery* means "a total or complete abandoning of one's principles." The word is made up on the word *ad*, meaning "to add" ... and the word *ulter*, meaning "other." It means "to add other" or to dilute by adding something else to a substance. There was a time not too long ago, before the kind of federal controls that have evolved to protect the consumer, that dairies would unscrupulously add water to milk to make it go further. Grocers were not above putting sand in the sugar, rocks in the beans, and water in the vinegar. Adulterate means to add something that cheapens the quality or upsets the completeness.

Literally *adultery* usually refers to sex relations outside of marriage. Judgments are made, based on moral codes and values that change with ages and cultures. For instance, a young girl said, "Sex is a perfectly natural activity, like eating or sleeping. Why should we treat it in any other way? Why all the taboos and prudery?" Of course, she is reacting to the rigid morals of her grandmother, who was probably wrong, for purity is not the same thing as prudery. Purity is a matter of consciousness. Prudery is simply a moralistic hangup. The prude may also have a strong sexual desire that is being repressed.

But the young girl is also wrong. For sex is not a thing ... but simply a way in which a person may express. If we deal with sex as a thing, we reduce ourselves to the level of animals. In its purest sense, adultery is not what two people do wrongly together, but what we do destructively to ourselves. We lose our sense of integrity.

Persons in or out of marriage who engage in "sex without love" are prostituting themselves, adulterating their true worth as persons. They are selling themselves short on the real meaning of life, which can be found only in the total communion of man and woman in the fullness of inner-centered love.

"Today there is a continuing discussion on the question of 'open marriage' and marriages where there is a commitment without the license. Of course, under the old moral code such relationships are condemned out of hand. However, even if it were agreed that such behavior is immoral, may it not be less moral for married persons to live together for sex, or out of obligation to the children, or by reason of society's taboo on divorce? In whatever way we view morality, is it not moral to be honest and immoral to lie? If two people are honest with themselves and each other in that they do not want the legal responsibilities of marriage, should they be considered less moral than two people who are living a lie in a marital façade behind which there is a psychological and spiritual separation?"(*Life Is For Loving*)

Let us go beyond the implications of morality to the insights of metamorality, beyond the narrow codes of religion to the "new insight in Truth." This seventh commandment articulates a law that is beautiful and wonderful. It is a tragedy that it has been so neglected and misunderstood. The emphasis has

always been placed on the sin or the physical acts
and personal relationships. The sin is not in the act,
but in the thought that leads to the act, and the adulteration of pure thought implied.

Jesus had little patience with the old traditions
that were so filled with prejudices and hypocrisy. He
shattered this commandment into its minute compo-
nents, again leaving no room to hide. And as a result
he lifted the "You shall not commit adultery" law out
of the purely prudish and moralistic frame in which
the pious Pharisees could condemn and stone to
death persons caught up in the web of human emotions. He said: *"You have heard that it was said, 'You
shall not commit adultery.' But I say to you that every one
who looks at a woman lustfully has already committed
adultery with her in his heart"* (Mt. 5:27).

This lifts the commandment to the level of divine
law, the law of consciousness. Traditionally, religion
has emphasized moral codes for conduct and judgments on immoral acts. There is no denying that the
seventh commandment has application on this level.
But more significantly, the act of adultery involves a
weakening or adulteration of one's own self-worth.
And it may be applied in a much broader sense as
dealing with the adulteration of Truth in the many
unthinking ways.

It could be said, for instance, that Judas was an
adulterer because he did not see the spiritual depth

in Jesus. He confused the Christ idea with temporal authority and material rewards. Of course, Judas was not alone in this. Few of the disciples saw much deeper than Judas, as evidenced by their swift disappearance in Jesus' time of great need. Peter had that one radiant moment when he cried out: *"You are the Christ, the Son of the living God"* (Mt. 16:16). However, he was soon back in adultery as he denied three times that he had even heard of the man, Jesus.

Whenever we see less than the Christ in another or in ourselves, we commit adultery. Does this surprise you? Again, there is no place to hide. For who of us sees the divine depth in people, all people, all the time? Does anyone? How often we adulterate the Truth in our thoughts about conditions or circumstances. We fail to see the allness of God, to know that the Lord God is One. We break the first as well as the seventh commandment.

No wonder Jesus said to those who were about to stone the woman "taken in adultery": *"Let him who is without sin among you be the first to throw a stone at her"* (Jn. 8:7). We may have thought that he was intimating that they were all having extramarital affairs. It is said that Jesus bent down and wrote with his finger on the ground. Some have speculated that the writing contained clues of secret trysts involving the Pharisee-accusers, which he knew by some psychic power. It could be. But it seems much more likely that Jesus was referring to the sins of the mind. In other words, he might have been saying, "If any of you is free from the sin of adulteration of Truth, of not seeing the best in people, let him stand up and administer the punishment to this unfortunate woman." With that criteria, who could throw a stone? Even if one of the accusers were free of mental sin up to that moment, by his act of accusation he was committing adultery right then.

The commandment is broad in its application to human thought. *"You shall not commit adultery."* You shall not adulterate reality by judging by appearances, and thus by adding on something other than the Truth. You shall not pollute that which is pure and holy by seeing in a mirror darkly. It is a large order. But then, it is law and not caprice that we are dealing with. It may seem to be an impossible restraint to be told, "Don't short-circuit the wires" or "Don't lean too far over the precipice." The child may think so. However, as adults, we know that the prohibition is in our own best interest.

When there is a greater awareness of the law of consciousness more and more people will be turned off by preachers or politicians who agonize over the decadence of modern society. We have been told for too long how sinful and perverse we are, and how our society is on the road to perdition. The world needs leaders who will begin with the principle, *"The*

Lord our God is one Lord," and who will encourage people by their optimism and faith to release their "imprisoned splendor," and thus collectively to bring about the *"kingdom on earth as it is in heaven."*

A few years ago a radio preacher was heard delivering an emotional sermon on the evils of dancing. He gave a long and lurid description of all the obscene things that were going on in the minds of the two people who were holding their bodies together on the dance floor. It was not enough that he was revealing the filthy state of his own mind, but he was polluting the airwaves with his adulterous rhetoric.

There is an Islamic legend about a man who had two sons. One of the sons was very pious, arising early every morning for his devotions, while the other brother slept on. One morning the pious one complained to his father that his brother was lost in irreligious slumber while he faithfully kept the spirit of the Quran. The father wisely replied, "Son of my soul, it would be better to remain in sleep than to awake to behold the faults of others." For this finding of fault is adultery.

The word *commit* of the commandment brings the matter of adultery right back squarely where it belongs, in the context of one's own actions. It literally means to send forth. It is something that takes place in the mind, as an attitude, a perception, a motivation, and then goes forth into some form of action.

When the attitude is negative and narrow, the action will be limited and self-destructive. The ideal, of course, is found in Psalm 37: *Commit your way to the Lord; trust in him, and he will act.* Commit yourself to Truth, send it forth in words of power, and you will be in the flow of the divine creative process. He will act.

In a very real sense you adulterate yourself whenever you tell a half-truth or stretch the truth in exaggeration. To say something about yourself or about another that is less than true morally, or even spiritually, is committing adultery. If you sell yourself short out of feelings of inferiority or for ulterior motives, you commit adultery. The word *ulterior* is interesting. It comes from the same root as *adultery*. If a person says one thing but intends another thing, we say he has an ulterior motive. This literally means an *ulter* or other motive. He adds *ulter* to the situation, which is the exact meaning of adultery.

An understatement also adulterates. How many persons are guilty of the self-put-down? Someone may ask about your performance at work or on the stage, "How did you do?" If you say "Oh, all right" or "Not very well" when you know you did very well, you are committing adultery. False humility is self-abasement. It is demeaning and adulterous.

A commonly used phrase today is "If you have it, flaunt it." It may come from ostentation or egotism, but the principle is valid. The word *flaunt* refers to that which comes out of the flow. We tend, however, to call attention to that which bubbles forth as being of our own doing, rather than as the divine creative process that is flowing through us. It is true, if you have it, "flow with it." Rejoice in it. Be proud of it. Accept it in the sense of affirming your self-worth.

And then if someone praises you for your performance, "That was magnificent!"—instead of demurring, "Oh, it wasn't anything," you can say, "Yes, it *was* good, wasn't it?" For you know that it came out of the flow, and you do not want to dilute it.

In other words, do not exaggerate when talking about yourself. But at the same time, do not minimize or belittle your abilities and achievements. When you catch the spirit of the third commandment, you will know that you have an obligation to call yourself by the name of the Lord. Then you will speak the Truth to and about yourself at all times. Anything less than the Truth of our oneness in the One is adultery.

If you speak words of Truth in prayer or in treatment, then later say "I sure hope it works!" and then go back to worrying, you are committing adultery. If you pray with "vain repetitions" or nagging affirmations or treatments after you have once made your commitment to a realization of Truth, you are committing adultery. Jesus said: *"In your prayers do not go babbling on like the heathen, who imagine that the more they say the more likely they are to be heard"* (Mt. 6:7, 8 NEB). Speak the word of Truth! Then let go. If you take hold of the problem again in fear and anxiety, there is evident disregard for the principle, a lack of trust in God, the One. This is committing adultery. Know the Truth about a person, an experience, a thing or a condition, and then say, "Amen!" Stop going over it again and again, trying to recreate the idea, to rephrase and revitalize the words you have formulated, begging, pleading, supplicating God for answers that are already yours in Mind. For this is committing adultery.

Make a new commitment to the flow of good. Determine that you will no longer pollute the atmosphere with negatives. "Commit your way unto the Lord." *The Lord* means the I AM. Send forth your I AM power: *"trust in him, and he will act."* Great manifestations of good will follow.

You always have a choice: Commit your way unto the Lord or commit adultery. Which shall it be? You will be faced with this dilemma scores of times every day of your life. Make the commitment to keep your thoughts on the high level of Truth. *Whatever is true ... honorable ... just ... pure ... lovely ... gracious ..* think about these things (Phil. 4:8). Send forth I AM power in positive words and actions or you will pollute your mind, body and affairs with habit patterns of inferiority, animosity and negation.

Make this commitment, and often: I will no longer commit adultery. I will not add other limiting aspects to the Truth. I will judge righteous judgment instead of judging by appearances. I will keep the purity of my consciousness through speaking and acting on positive ideas and creative images. And I have faith that this integrity of consciousness will lead me to integrity in all my relations and affairs.

The
EIGHTH
Commandment

You shall not steal (Ex. 20:15).

This would appear to be the most needed commandment in our day, for it deals with respect for property and right of ownership. It is reported that all kinds of stealing, which includes shoplifting and employee theft as well as armed robbery, amounts to well over $30 billion a year. This is more than double the combined cost of education in the whole country, including buildings, salary and equipment.

On top of this we could add the tremendous cost of insurance against theft, and the cost of security measures of all kinds. We could also include such equally pernicious kinds of stealing as stretching breaks and lunch hours, falsified sick-days, padded expense accounts and reduced effort or productivity.

Of course, someone has to pay for all this. We the people do. It is the great rip-off.

What can be done? We have emphasized laws and locks and police protection. It is generally agreed today that such measures have done little to handle, let alone cut down, the problem. They actually add to the public burden.

In Moses' time the "no stealing" law was enforced very simply and realistically. If a man who stole an ox was caught, he had to repay the owner with five oxen. There were not many thieves in Israel and no jails. Stealing did not pay. Paying back five times what one had been caught stealing was a real deterrent.

Under our juridical system, let us say a man steals a suit. He is arrested, tried, found guilty, and put in jail for six months. Or, even worse, because of the backlog of court cases, he may wait trial for six months. To ease the jam, he is allowed to plea bargain, which means to confess to a lesser charge. Finally, he is convicted on a misdemeanor charge, slapped on the wrist, and discharged.

Note what happens. The man who lost the suit not only does not recover the suit, but he might have to sacrifice many days' work while appearing in court as a witness. Society loses the benefit of the victim's work, and bears the cost of the arrest, trial, and imprisonment of the thief. Everyone loses, and possibly the thief loses least of all.

Under Mosaic law, the man caught stealing the suit would have to go to work and restore four additional suits of clothes to the owner. Unbelievably simple! Actually, a pilot program of this kind is now being conducted in Connecticut. Persons convicted of crime will be required to pay back their victims. More and more people are agreeing that this is a more rational sentence than sending them to jail or putting them on probation. The goal is to take the profit out of crime.

If properly administered, such a program would insure that by the time the thief finishes earning the repayment, he may well have learned that when a person steals, he not only makes a rip in the fabric of society that must be repaired, but he steals from himself. Until this is realized, no laws will be effective. One must be made to realize, in a human as well as spiritual sense, that the only rip-off is a self-rip-off.

It is ignorance of the law of compensation that leads people on the endless round of trying to get something for nothing, hoping for the lucky break, or finding the shortcut to advancement. It is this limited view that motivates the thief, the gambler and the compulsive speculator.

We have repeatedly stressed that the Mosaic law was intended for near-primitive people. Certainly, infants need playpens, children need fenced-in yards, and teenagers may require curfews. Adults, too, may need the reminders of "Keep Out," "Keep Off the Grass," and "No Smoking."

However, children must be readied for life by making all restraints progressively unnecessary as they develop what Tennyson calls *self-reverence, self-knowledge, and self-control.* For if the person refrains from stealing only because he is afraid of being caught, he is harboring a grave limitation of consciousness. As with the seventh commandment, he has already broken the spiritual law. Moral restraints are a step along the way, but only with an understanding of metamorality can we begin to solve the basic human need. Little Skippy once remarked, "I don't worry about it, 'cause I think too much of my mind." When the shortcut of stealing becomes literally unthinkable because we are respectful of the swift judgment of mind-action, then we understand metamorality.

The child needs to be taught what true integrity is by the example of his adult models: his parents, teachers, and religious, political and business leaders. He must be exposed to discipline that is sure and just. This will lead to the dawning awareness that one cannot really steal—ever. He who robs another, robs himself first. He makes a break in his own integrity or wholeness at the expense of his own ultimate

good. He must be led to the overwhelming conclusion that one can never get something for nothing.
In school we have an obligation to help him to understand that one who may cheat on an examination
may pass the test, but that the purpose of the test is
not to limit him, but to enrich him. By cheating he
denies himself the enrichment that the course was
intended to bring. He steals from himself the good
that should have been his but that never can be so
long as he fails to keep the law of integrity.

The Greek philosopher Zeno once said that the
most important part of learning is to unlearn our
errors. It is vital that every person should unlearn the
erroneous belief in luck or favoritism in life or in the
universe. There is a legitimate, royal abundance for
every living soul; but there is a price to pay. Create
the conditions in consciousness that will make the
result inevitable. When the pattern is formed in
mind, the result will flow forth—and no matter what
the observers may say, there is no luck involved.

Another great error that must be unlearned is that
life is lived from the outside-in. Under this fallacious
belief, the whole purpose of life is to go out into the
world to get learning, to get friends, and to get
money and things. When our whole cultural system
is built around the idea of "get, get, get," it is little
wonder that "getting there" becomes the universal
goal. Under the "success syndrome," the means of

getting there are too often justified if the ethics are slightly in the "gray area." We have a tendency to glamorize the sophisticated criminal because he got there! Success is not just getting there. It is earning the right to *be* there. There is a law of consciousness involved. And we fail to acknowledge it when we talk of luck, or knowing the right people, or pulling strings, or even of having the right image.

Life is lived from within-out. That which every person hungers for is really within himself. It is not the acquisition of glitter and glamour of the world, but the release of his own "imprisoned splendor." We must unlearn the concept of "get, get, get" and become enthusiastic about the ideal of "give, give, give." If a child grows up under the influence of this kind of philosophy, stealing-thoughts would be "unthinkable."

Ralph Waldo Emerson says that people take such great care that their neighbor shall not cheat them, but there will come a time when they will be more concerned that they do not cheat their neighbor. When one really understands the spiritual law of "You shall not steal," he becomes meticulously careful not to take or accept anything that is not rightfully his ... or fail to fulfill an obligation that is.

Here is an experience that happens in one way or another every day. Suppose when paying your check in a restaurant, you suddenly realize that the cashier has given you too much change. What to do? If the focus of your thought is on "getting," you could easily rationalize this as a divine outworking and as a repayment for other times when you may have been shortchanged. And, after all, who would know? However, when you know the divine law—that you can never get something for nothing—the decision is easy. Out of your giving consciousness you call it to the cashier's attention immediately. When you know that there is always a price to pay, why subject yourself to a cost that may not be to your liking? You would, in that small way, lose control of the forces that are working in and through and around you. It is not worth it.

There was a story in the news some years ago about a man who came upon a Brink's bag that had fallen unnoticed out of the armored truck. The bag contained half a million dollars in small denomination bills, unmarked and untraceable. Without any hesitation he called the authorities and turned it in. He tells how his life was made miserable for months by people who asked him angrily, "Why did you turn it in?" They seemed to be saying, "We the underprivileged of society had this one chance of getting back. But you blew it! No one would ever have known." His steady reply: "But I would know!" He had his integrity, which meant more to him than any instant fortune.

"You shall not steal" then means, in a deeper sense, "You shall not take or try to hold something that does not belong to you, that has not come to you by right of consciousness." Any attempt to circumvent this cosmic law is mental theft even if it is perfectly legal. True, it may sometimes appear that others have achieved success even in illegal or unethical ways. The Bible says: *"Vengeance is mine, and recompense"* (Deut. 32:35). This refers not to the big man "out there," who looks on and makes notes in his black book, but to the inexorable working of divine law. In the end everyone must "pay the piper"! Jesus said: *"What is that to you? Follow me!"* (Jn. 21:22). You have your own integrity to uphold, your own relationship with divine law to maintain.

Some persons tend to lose this perspective when it comes to prayer. It is but a transcendent shortcut to their good, a matter of pulling divine strings. It is well to remember that God can do no more for you than He can do through you. There is no way that, through prayer, God can be influenced to give you some blessing for which you have not earned the right in consciousness. To be healthy, one must have a health-consciousness. To be prosperous, one must have a prosperity-consciousness. To "make it" one must have what it takes, which is slang for the consciousness that attracts. To attempt, through prayer, to acquire something that you have not earned the right for, is a kind of stealing. True prayer seeks nothing from God, for God has already given us all. *"It is your Father's good pleasure to give you the kingdom"* (Lk. 12:32). Prayer seeks only to let go and let the divine flow unfold, knowing that the readiness to receive depends on the ability to give. Give way ... and give thanks! Then "move your feet" with full faith in the divine flow.

How important it is to get the realization that every person is constantly and abundantly supported by an all-providing universe, just as surely and beautifully as the lily of the field! There is never a need to go out to get it or take it. *"Consider the lilies ... they neither toil nor spin; yet I tell you, even Solomon in all his glory was not arrayed like one of these"* (Mt. 6:28, 29). The lily could never steal or even be tempted to do so, for how could it ask for anything more?

It is true that things and money come to us from the world "out there." But true wealth is not the things. It is the magnetic flow of Spirit within us that draws the things. A magnet attracts and holds iron filings. An unmagnetized piece of steel not only does not attract anything, but even if filings are piled upon it, they will fall off at the first jostling. This is not favoritism, or good or bad luck. It is the working of fundamental law. Stealing of any kind comes out of the desire to get or achieve something in ignorance of the basic law of attraction.

One of the most important discoveries to be made in the quest for Truth is that the greatest sense of fulfillment in life is not in what the magnet may attract, but in the inner sense of wholeness that comes from just being in the flow, which then is only outwardly experienced as the power to draw things and the things that are drawn. Some persons may live a long time before they make this discovery. They work year after frustrating year to pile the iron filings on the unmagnetized steel. They may joke about "easy come, easy go," but it covers a deep inner feeling of hurt and frustration.

Jesus put it succinctly: *"But seek first his kingdom and his righteousness, and all these things shall be yours as well"* (Mt. 6:33). It is but another way of saying, Get yourself into the flow of the divine creative process and create the conditions within your own mind that will make the outward manifestation inevitable. Turn from the goals of *getting* and *having* to the ideal of *giving* and *being*.

Your education is never complete until you really understand the law of consciousness: Whatever happens to you, whatever happens around you, will be in accord with that which is within you, your own state of mind. And whatever is in your consciousness must happen, no matter who may try to stop it. On the other hand, whatever is not in your consciousness cannot happen. Of course, you can change your consciousness. And that is what this new insight in Truth is all about.

It is likely that everyone, at some time in his life, has been tempted to take a shortcut to achievement or acquisition. It could have involved anything from a slight "fudging" on a report to actions that were completely illegal. One may feel guilty that he had the temptation even if he wisely held back. However, the dishonest or immoral aspect is only part of the problem. In consciousness there was a feeling of lack, of envy, and the negative desire to retaliate against an unjust society. This is the root cause that will lead to the "comeback" of many unforeseen problems. One may get by with the slight or even major indiscretion, but in the ledger of cosmic balance, there is a debit that must ultimately be accounted for.

What to do about such things? If there is a need, no matter how desperate, instead of trying to "get" by any means, the ideal would be to start giving. Someone once said, "When things get tight, something has to give!" In the long run the only way to overcome the tendency or even the temptation to look for shortcuts to acquisition or achievement is to learn how to give. Think "give" instead of "get."

One of the most pathetic figures of the Bible is the young man of means who wanted to "have eternal life." He asked what he should do. Jesus said that he should keep the commandments, naming a few of them: *"You shall not kill; You shall not commit adultery; You shall not steal; You shall not bear false witness; Honor your father and mother; and, You shall love your neighbor as yourself"* (Mt. 19:18, 19). The young man said that he had observed the commandments all his life. Jesus said that there was one more thing lacking: *"Go, sell what you possess and give to the poor ... and come follow me"* (Mt. 19:21-22). The young man was crestfallen. He went away sorrowful; for he had great possessions.

The inference of the story is that this fine young man, who was obviously very religious, had a disqualifying lack in consciousness. Jesus sensed that the young man was bound in personal possession. He did not really have great possessions, his possessions had him. He may have come into his wealth by inheritance, or he may have amassed it through his acquisitive drive. However, his life was being lived from the outside. He had no sense of the flow of substance. He did not know that one never really owns anything. Consciousness draws substance that is ours to shape and set in motion, but we are never more than stewards of the flow, which is always of God. Any attempt to have and to hoard material things is evidence of lack of the consciousness by which it may be held, thus we are breaking the eighth commandment.

There is an old adage, "You never really own anything unless you can give it away." This was the test to which Jesus was subjecting the young man. If he could have given it all to the poor, then he would not have needed to. That he could not do it indicated that what he owned was not really his by right of consciousness. It would always be a millstone around his neck. It is a stern law, but an inexorable one.

Great responsibility goes along with wealth and possessions of all kinds. Many persons in the practice of the prosperity laws of Truth have given prime emphasis to "demonstrating" abundance. It is a valid aspect of the new insight in Truth. However, one thing that is not always clearly understood is that it matters not that affluence has been achieved in perfectly legal and ethical ways; to hold it in possessiveness, and to fail to use the substance rightly in a commitment to giving is to break the eighth commandment.

The "back to the Ten Commandments" people insist that the problems of crime and immorality would be solved if more people would heed the eighth commandment: *"You shall not steal!"* Of course. It is like saying that we would have more grass in the parks if people would just obey the "Keep Off the Grass" signs. The fact is, the grass will be spared when people become more aware of the underlying Truth that "you cannot steal," for your life is totally entwined with the inexorable laws of the universe. When more people discover that the only practical and fulfilling way to live is to live to give instead of to receive, metamorality will become the rule.

Jesus said: *"Give, and it will be given to you"* (Lk. 6:38). The divine flow within you requires but one thing of you: your consent or willingness to be a receiving channel. It is like the water faucet that must be opened to the flow in order that water may pour forth freely. Jesus is simply stressing the need to get into a giving consciousness in order to sustain a continuity of the flow of good in your life. With the emphasis on giving, there is little likelihood that your mind may turn to shortcuts to getting, or in worrying about keeping. Honesty, integrity and respect for the property of others will be as natural to you as breathing.

When you think "give" instead of "get" you will experience the "life more abundant" that Jesus idealizes. In your work, your play, your relationships and your church, think "give"! Think of your work as giving. Think of every relationship as an opportunity to give. Give to your family. Give to your neighbors. Give to your community. Give to the nation. Think give. Give way to the divine flow.

The faucet is opened so that it can give, and the more it gives, the greater the flow by which to give. It is important to understand this great ideal: The purpose of giving is not to receive but to give. The moment we focus on receiving, we begin to lose the flow of giving. At this point, in a relative sense, we begin to engage in stealing. Jesus said: *"Do not let your left hand know what your right hand is doing"* (Mt. 6:3). This simply means, "Don't let your acquisitive instinct influence your giving, so that the gift is tainted with self." Give to give to give yet more. In this consciousness, you can be certain that you are "breaking" the eighth commandment out of its static shell and keeping its spirit in the highest possible way.

The
NINTH
Commandment

You shall not bear false witness against your neighbor (Ex. 20:16).

The fabric of any society is composed of the interlacing of human relations. The preservation of that fabric calls for certain self-evident ethical standards that are implied in the ninth commandment. Don't tell lies about people ... Don't exaggerate ... Don't engage in excessive criticism. It is said, "A man's word is his bond." If we cannot count on the word of our neighbor, then the ties that bind us together as a society are perilously loosened.

In its first layer of meaning the ninth commandment sets forth the principle of the sacredness of the judicial system. The word *bear* means "to answer." In court, whether as plaintiff, defendant or witness, a person must speak "the truth, the whole truth, and nothing but the truth" in a charge involving his neighbor. A lie is a false witness, whether told to help or to convict someone.

In a courtroom today, the testimony of a witness may convict a person or set him free. It could even send him to his death. However, when the witness gives his testimony, he has no further responsibility. If there is a conviction, the courts administer the punishment. It was not so in olden times. Under Mosaic law, when a sentence was pronounced on an accused person, the witnesses against him had to carry out the sentence. If he was to be stoned to death, the accusers and witnesses had to do the stoning. It was a strong deterrent against false witnessing.

Also a provision carried over from the ancient Code of Hammurabi (a king of Babylon, ca. 2000 BCE): If a witness was found to have given a false testimony, he would receive the punishment that would have gone to the accused. Thus the accuser literally staked his life on his words. It was dangerous to lie.

The word *witness* comes from an old English word, *witan*, meaning "understanding," "intelligence," "wisdom." It is related to the Sanskrit *Veda*, which is the name of the sacred scriptures of Hinduism. It is also the root of *vedanta*, the chief philosophy among the Hindus. The word *witness* implies "seeing," "knowing," or what we call "consciousness."

There are different kinds of witnessing: ear-witness, eye-witness and heart-witness. In legal cases much is made of the fact that a witness saw something. "Seeing is believing" is the axiom. Actually, the opposite is truer, "Believing is seeing." It is much easier to see a person doing something dishonest if one believes he is a thief. What one sees and hears is strongly influenced by consciousness. Note, for instance, how a person afflicted with paranoia may see and hear all sorts of wrongs being done around him or to him.

When you know that "life is consciousness," you know that you have a responsibility for what you see and hear and sense. You always see according to your level of awareness. The seeing thus implies a judgment. You are not responsible for what people do or say, but you *are* responsible for what you do or say or think about them. You cannot change them, but it is your mind, and thus you can change your thoughts. You can change the attitudes you hold toward them and your intentions of dealing with them.

As you break through the crystallized shell of the ninth commandment, the first discovery is that you really cannot bear false witness. The reason? What you say or report on expresses where you are and what you are. When you bear witness to error, you reveal an awareness of error, perhaps a preoccupation with error, in your own consciousness. As Walt Whitman said: *The good or bad you say of another, you actually say of yourself.* If everyone really understood this, most negative criticism and gossip would be eliminated, and bridge clubs and coffee breaks might lose their reason for existence.

Consciousness being what it is, our dealing with negative things about others, whether true or untrue, not only bears witness to our own state of consciousness, but it opens the way to its outpicturing in us. The principle of causation that is implied is this: What you say about another person will happen to you, for by saying it you indicate that it has already happened in you. This is what Jesus had in mind as he said: *"Judge not, that you be not judged. For with the judgment you pronounce you will be judged, and the measure you give will be the measure you get"* (Mt. 7:1-2).

A strong implication of the ninth commandment is criticism. Listen to the conversation in a typical social gathering, and even though it may be judgmental, use this measuring device: Great minds talk about ideas, average minds talk about events, and small minds talk about people. You may be shocked. Even more, you will note that the conversation about people will invariably be in a critical vein.

Why do you criticize? Usually it evidences poor self-regard, and it is a subconscious attempt to cut the other person down to a size where the critic can feel more comfortable in relating. If you really want to work with this ninth commandment, you might spend one week checking up on your tendency to criticize. When you are on the verge of saying something about a person, use the classic test: Is it true? Is it kind? Is it needful? You may well discover that, in most cases, what you are about to say with enthusiasm might much better be left unsaid.

The word *criticism* comes from a Greek word coined by Aristotle. It means "to evaluate or establish true worth." Obviously, the original meaning has been lost. For it was intended to mean not faultfinding, but looking for the good. In this sense, it is as wrong not to creatively criticize one you love as to destructively criticize anyone.

Senator Paul Douglas once told how he had long had trouble with his opponents. One day at a Quaker meeting a man said, "Whenever someone differs with you or criticizes you, try to show him in every way that you love him." Douglas knew that, as the Quakers put it, "the man had spoken to his condition." He had long been meeting criticism with retaliation. So he decided that he would no longer oppose people as people, but he would simply oppose ideas. He would never attack a person's character, but always try to show goodwill toward his adversaries. He said that his rise in politics began when he heard the words of the Quaker man, and did something about them.

Bearing false witness against your neighbor is criticizing him to put him down rather than to build him up. Instead of trying to help him, it is helping yourself to feel more adequate at his expense. The commandments are not saying, "Don't do that, for it is not nice!" They deal with cosmic law. And in this case, by bearing false witness, you are setting up negative causes for which you will have to pay the price.

There is an interesting Christian fundamentalist term, "witness for Christ." It might imply proselytizing, standing on street corners to preach the Gospel, or standing up in a revival meeting to give personal testimony. However, this term takes on a whole new meaning when you realize that Christ is not Jesus, but the divinity within Jesus, a divinity that is also within every person. It means knowledge of the Christ indwelling, your very own divine potential ... and seeing from that knowledge, hearing from that knowledge, and feeling from that knowledge ... and then projecting it in the words you speak, the things you do, and the feelings you engender.

Jesus said: *"For this I was born, and for this I have come into the world, to bear witness to the truth"* (Jn. 18:37). We have been misled into thinking that this was "very God" telling us that he was a special dispensation of infinite Mind. Overlooked are his clearly stated words, "All that I do you can do too." Actually, every person has his own inner relationship with the divine flow. Jesus was only saying of himself what every person can and ultimately must say of himself: Everyone came into the world to bear witness to the Truth of his own being.

Does this mean that each person must preach or teach? No! Truth is not the spiritual "gems" we mouth. Truth is a nonverbal reality. We experience Truth in the depths of our being and then we attempt to articulate the experience; we encode into words that which is basically a feeling. To bear witness to Truth is to know who we are and to express our true selves honestly.

The Truth of you is the Christ of you. Do you really know this Christ self? Is this the level of you that you are bearing witness to? Or are you bearing false witness to your neighbor?

We are civilized creatures, and civilization has often come to mean the responsibility of putting on a façade, wearing a mask under the guise of being "normal" or "decent" or "socially acceptable." A child in a religious family is taught at an early age that he must be good or he will be flogged, so he puts on the mask of "goodness" and "morality." He goes off to school where he learns to don the mask of erudition and intellectual maturity. We also wear masks of culture, masks of urbanity, and many masks that consist of little more than the clothes we wear and the makeup we painstakingly apply.

The greatest fear of the average person is that someone will catch him unawares without his mask. This is classically demonstrated in the following vignette: A little girl comes home telling her mother that the new neighbor is coming over to visit. Mother excitedly runs around the house picking up the papers, hanging up clothes, and straightening the rugs and furniture. The little girl, surprised, says, "But mama, she is just our neighbor!" To which the mother replies, "Do you think I want my neighbor to think that our house always looks the way it always looks?" Thus her orderly house would bear false witness to her neighbor.

In Arthur Miller's *Death of a Salesman*, we have the tragic story of one who is so concerned with being well-liked that he never discovers who he is or how to be himself. In his early years he learned to "win friends and influence people" as a salesman by putting on a mask of geniality. However, behind this façade was the empty shell of a man who had never really known life as a quest, an unfoldment. The most important thing to him was to be well-liked, but he did not really like himself. When his employer terminated his services, he did not have the capacity to let go and walk on. There was nothing to go to, because he really had nothing to go *from*. His life was over!

The interesting thing is that Willy Loman was bearing false witness only because he thought he was. As Emerson says, we do not represent but misrepresent ourselves. Willie rejected himself and put on a façade of dash and self-assurance, but he never knew that the person he tried so hard to be was the person he really was. At any time through the years he could have removed the mask and "let his light shine," and his effectiveness as a salesman and as a person would have been enhanced. The false witness was not the fact that he was playing a game, but that he thought he was.

There is a folktale about a great ruler who was hard and cruel and whose face had become lined with ugliness. He fell in love with a beautiful princess whom he wanted to be his queen. However, ashamed of his grim appearance, he had his magicians create for him a mask of thin wax that carefully followed his own features but made him look kind and pleasant. He married the girl and had many years of happiness, during which time his character and consciousness underwent a complete metamorphosis. However, he began to feel pangs of conscience because of his deception. Finally, he decided that he had to be true to himself and his lovely wife. He removed the mask. And, miracle of miracles, he discovered that he had actually become in fact and feature the kind, honest and good person that he had played at being. In a very real sense, the false witness that he was bearing to his subjects was the hard and cruel manner that he had projected before he met his lovely princess, which is symbolic of finding the Christ within.

Many persons become interested in personal development through the study of this new insight in Truth. The word *develop* does not mean to create something out of nothing, as many have supposed. It is not putting on a façade that is manufactured by affirmations and autosuggestion. The word comes from the same root as *envelope*. To develop, then, means to unwrap, to unfold, to release and use that which is already available within. Whatever you desire to become you already are, for your desire is an intuitive foreshadowing of the inner reality.

"Know the truth, and the truth will make you free!" Free from the limitations of the past, free from the sham of human consciousness that forever tries to obscure what you are, and free from the false attitude that believes that what you are is not good enough. Knowing Truth should also set you free from the ego needs to emphasize the years of your study, the teachers you have worked with, and the degrees you have achieved. It was Jesus who said that you are to be known by the fruits of your consciousness. Any claims of spiritual excellence, not borne out by evidence of mastery, is bearing false witness.

To truly keep the ninth commandment calls for humility, the self-honesty to see yourself as a lifelong student on the quest. The need is to see oneself in right relations to the divine flow. Nowhere is this process more articulately summed up than in the closing lines of the Lord's Prayer as it is commonly spoken: *For Thine is the Kingdom*—all right ideas, plans, purposes come out of infinite Mind; *And the Power*—the strength and creative ability to put them into operation comes from the divine flow; *And the Glory*—thus all credit of accomplishment belongs to God.

When we truly understand this process, we will keep ourselves humbly receptive to the divine flow. We will be true to ourselves in giving witness for the Christ pattern within. In this consciousness we will never be untrue to anyone else. We will be too big to belittle, too secure to be critical, and too humble to be boastful. This is why Jesus emphasized "love your neighbor," for when you are loving you are living fully and receptively, you are in tune with God, and in right relation with your fellow human beings.

Every person is a steward of the tiny spark of living fire that one may desecrate but never quite lose. You are like a lighthouse keeper. You have the continuing responsibility of keeping the light trim and burning bright. *"You are the light of the world,"* said Jesus. *"Let your light ... shine"* (Mt. 5:14, 16). The smile of your face and the friendliness of your manner are contagious. Walk down the street of your town with a friendly smile and you will leave a "mile of smiles" behind you.

From a moral point of view you are charged not to bear false witness to your neighbor. From the perspective of metamorality you have a responsibility, as an integral part of the universe in which you coexist with your neighbor, to radiate to him your witness for Truth. *"He who loves his brother abides in the light, and in it there is no cause for stumbling. But he who hates his brother is in the darkness and walks in the darkness, and does not know where he is going, because the darkness has blinded his eyes"* (1 Jn. 2:10, 11).

It is relatively easy to refrain from bearing false witness to your neighbor in a moral sense, but to really express your Christ-self to your neighbors of the world calls for total commitment. It means revising all your thoughts about yourself, and changing your way of thinking, seeing, feeling, speaking and acting. It means a complete purification of consciousness.

In biblical times this commitment of purification was symbolized by the act of going into a pool or a river to bathe. Originally, what is now a rite of baptism was done for sanitary purposes. For people who rarely bathed, it indicated a commitment to make a clean breast of things. Certainly, one who is physically unclean or who has unpleasant body odors is bearing false witness to the "temple of the living God."

The bathing process is an excellent symbol to work with, the ideal of a spiritual as well as a physical cleansing. Every morning or evening as you take your bath or shower, close your eyes for a few moments and identify the experience as an immersion or baptism in the allness of God. Get the feeling that all that is impure is being washed away, and that you are established in the dynamic flow of infinite life, love and intelligence. Make your commitment to keep your mind stayed on God, your whole being consciously in the flow of life. Resolve to bear witness to the Truth in mind, body and affairs.

The world today desperately needs people who will make the commitment to bear witness to the Truth, people who will make a special effort to be true to their God-self within, to be morally straight and metamorally disciplined. When there are more business people who are committed to honest representation of their products, more politicians who mean what they say, and more educators who set examples as well as examinations for their students, then truly we will begin to realize the millennium of God's kingdom, on earth as it is in heaven.

However, let us not at this point slip out of the commitment. For it is not "they" who are the problem. The problem is countless people ... and you are people. You make the difference! Or you can. Begin this moment to let your light shine, and to bear witness to the Truth.

The
TENTH
Commandment

*You shall not covet your neighbor's house;
you shall not covet your neighbor's wife, or
his man-servant, or his maid-servant, or
his ox, or his ass, or anything that is your
neighbor's* (Ex. 20:17).

A s we have observed in considering the Ten
Commandments up to this point, there are
many layers of meaning. From a purely moral point
of view the commandments are codes for improving
conduct and also for changing character. However,
from a metamoral point of view they contain hidden
keys for modifying consciousness.

To break through to the inner meaning of the tenth
commandment, we must rescue the word *covet* from
its totally negative implication. It is an interesting
word, coming from the same root as *cupid*. It means
love or passion. In modern usage covetousness

means inordinately desirous, greedy, avaricious. However, in the purest sense, the sin is not in coveting, but in that which is coveted.

In the Beatitudes, true to his form as an iconoclast, Jesus turns this commandment around: *"Blessed are those who hunger and thirst for righteousness, for they shall be satisfied"* (Mt. 5:6). In a very real sense this means "blessed are those who covet righteousness."

To covet means to desire, to long for, to want passionately—which of itself is certainly not wrong. If we are established in the consciousness of the first commandment, summed up most effectively in the words of the Shema, "The Lord God is One," then we covet the realization of oneness, and we *should* do so. We covet the inner kingdom and desire with all our hearts to get in the flow, and this, too, is an important state of consciousness. The promise is: Hunger and thirst for oneness with the flow, and you will be filled. Positive covetousness!

The great tragedy of humanity is the delusion that life is lived from outside-in. Our whole conditioning from infancy onward is to believe that whatever it is that we may want or need, it is "out there." It becomes a fixation: the love we hunger for will come with the right person; the guidance we seek may be found in some book or course of study or psychic or seer; the health we desire may be ours in the different climate or the new diet or from the charismatic healer. Also, we hunger and thirst (covet) for the car, the house, the job, the marriage partner, all "out there"—not really for their sake, but for what we are deluded they will bring us: acceptance as "a virile male," "an attractive woman," "a successful business person," etc. But unfortunately the very act of coveting things "out there" shuts us off from the inner flow.

This is why Jesus insisted that the rich young man needed to let go of his accumulations, or at least prove his willingness to do so. For unless he could give them up, he did not really possess them—he was being possessed by them. It is an important test to give ourselves in relation to our own accumulations: "Do I really have these things? Or do they have me?"

One of the negative by-products of Western materialism is that money has become the goal of human existence—a god that is worshiped and coveted. It could be said that most personal and international conflicts arise out of envy, jealousy and selfishly desiring that which belongs to others—normally money or that which is made possible by money.

This covetousness is creatively exploited by promoters, advertisers and motivational researchers—a whole industry devoted to getting people to covet things enough to go out and buy (usually on credit) what they can ill-afford and do not need. Every home contains many items that are the fruits of covetousness, which came out of overbuying to gain "middle-class prestige," or to cater to an inordinate passion to possess, and reflecting a deep sense of inadequacy or insufficiency. Covetousness, when centered in the external of life, is a kind of "mental gluttony."

This commandment, *"You shall not covet,"* was intended as a restraining fence to morally inhibit one who has not become spiritually aware. It says, "You must not look out into the world for your good." But as the person becomes spiritually mature, he discovers that the flow of his good is from within. Now he does not refrain from looking hungrily "out there" just because the commandment prohibits it, or because God is saying "No! No!" He knows that there is an abundance for all. "One God, one substance, one creative Mind, one perfect life." And he is always and forever one with that One. The moral restraint gives way to a metamoral commitment.

In the rich lore of the East there is a story of a teacher who wanted to demonstrate the need to "hunger and thirst for righteousness." He took his student out into the ocean and thrust his head under the water, holding it there until his lungs were bursting. The teacher let him up, and while the student gasped for air, he was asked, "When you were under water, what did you want more than anything else?" "Air," cried the student, "I wanted air!" "Then," said the teacher, "when you want the experience of God as you just now wanted air, you will experience the awakening."

The ideal of the tenth commandment is not so much to stop coveting, but to turn the focus of our attention from the without to the within. Our desire to *have* becomes a desire to *be*. We hunger and thirst, not for things, or power, or the titillation of the senses, but for a merging of the self with the divine flow—not for someone to possess and be loved by, but for a fulfilling release of the flow of love.

The Truth is, there is a divine action within that is always working to reveal to us and express *through* us that which makes for prosperity and fulfillment. Jesus said it clearly: *"It is your Father's good pleasure to give you the kingdom"* (Lk. 12:32). Your desire for any good thing is your intuitive feeling that it is already prepared for you if you can just "let." But when your mind turns to envy of others and to coveting what they have, the tendency is to frustrate the natural flow within yourself.

The coveting of things or power or relationships "out there" is like getting caught up in shadows. For what you see in the lives of others is the result of the flow of God through them. Where you see great creativity or power or wealth in the life of another person, it should give you hope that there is a flow. What

God *has* done, God *can* do. Or, as we sing, "What He's done for others, He can do for you."

Whenever you feel the twinges of covetousness, or jealousy, it is an intuitive sense of the divine action knocking at the door of your consciousness. It is saying, "I am here. Let me come in." Recall the allegory of Revelation: *"Behold, I stand at the door and knock; if any one hears my voice and opens the door, I will come in to him and eat with him, and he with me"* (Rev. 3:20).

There is abundance for all. It is like the shining of the sun. Every person in all the world can sun himself and there is enough for all. The supply of God is infinite and limitless. That which you see "out there," wherever or whatever it is, you can demonstrate in your own life, if you are willing to furnish the consciousness through which it may appear.

Instead of centering your attention "out there," which gives rise to the inordinate desire to have it for yourself, get your thought centered within yourself, realizing that the kingdom of God, the all-sufficient resource, is within you. Set about building the consciousness by which you can accept that which you find yourself desiring.

If covetousness has been a problem with you, turn to Jesus' Sermon on the Mount and read Matthew, Chapter 6, verses 25-34. In this amazing treatise he says, if you are overly concerned about things "out there," look to the birds of the air and the lilies of the field. Note how easily and abundantly they are supported. Should we assume that we are less important than they are in the divine plan? *"But seek first his kingdom and his righteousness, and all these things shall be yours as well"* (Mt. 6:33). Very simply this means: Seek first to know who you are, to disidentify yourself from beliefs in limitation and inadequacy, to get the realization that you are a child of God, heir to all the fullness of the divine flow. When you are centered in that flow, all that you have yearned for in the world will come to you ... and even more.

There is another aspect of this commandment that could easily be neglected. As students of this new insight in Truth we may assume that we are beyond materialistic covetousness, for we are working with spiritual law. But there is a great deal of "metaphysical coveting." This comes through the widespread materialization of the spiritual laws of prosperity. Through techniques of "demonstration" it is assumed that one can have anything he can "treat" for. There is a subtle rationalization of our old covetous ways, simply "putting new wine into old wineskins." We may well be on the same old path of coveting everything we see. Of course, now we feel very righteous about the fact that we are working with spiritual law to acquire the things. And since we are heirs to God's kingdom, it is right that we have anything and everything! Or so we feel.

This is not to say that we cannot achieve our goals in this way. For we certainly can demonstrate the cars, furs, diamonds and marriages that we pray for. However, if these things are realized without a recentering of our consciousness, they may well come forth at the *expense* of our spiritual growth, and not at its *expanse*.

It is like riding the merry-go-round where we clutch for the brass ring, which entitles us to a free ride, on which we clutch for more brass rings to have still more rides. There may be a restless urge to be where the action is ... and we are deluded by the playing of the calliope that the center of life is on the whirling carousel. And yet secretly we long to get off and walk on, in the full experience of life and growth. How sad it is that, for many persons in the materialistic emphasis of metaphysical study, spiritual growth is equated with the demonstration of things.

In our Western culture we are conditioned with a competitive view of life. All through our growth years we are made to compete: for grades in school, for jobs, for advancement, for awards and recognition. And the motivational researchers plan whole sales campaigns around this competitive theme. They say, in effect, "If you drive this car, you will be looked up to. You will be better than others."

This same competitive feeling carries over into our spiritual seeking. Students are often motivated to "make demonstrations" to keep up with the demonstrations the Joneses have made. Every student might be well advised to reflect on the wisdom of the axiom, "Seek not to be superior to other persons, but to be superior to your former self." In other words, get off the competitive treadmill.

It is a natural human tendency to want what another person has. This influence may be seen all through life as the person evolves from the infant to the adult: he desires the rattle ... or the wagon ... or the school grades ... or the jobs ... or the salaries ... or the marriage ... or the retirement benefits of others. It is a continuing cycle of covetousness. What we need to realize is that the envy is caused by the desire to *be like* the other, for we think that what he *has* is the reason for what he *is*. You cannot *be* someone else ... or even be *like* him. You can only *be* you. You can never be happy in any situation based on imitation.

It is this aspect of covetousness that leads to conformity, to acquiescence in the mores and styles and standards of the day, reducing our lives to dull monotones. So we slavishly fall in step with all the fads and current "rages." Covetousness thus becomes uninventiveness. Man is a creative creature, but envy and covetousness lead to a loss of originality, uniqueness and creativity.

So a very important facet of the tenth commandment, when it is broken down, is this: Don't try to be like others. Be original! Be you! You will always be a far greater success as *you* than as the best possible imitation of anyone else.

We tend to follow the patterns of the world because we have believed that life is to be found "out there," fulfillment is to be experienced "out there," love will come along "out there," and money and success are to be achieved "out there." There is a ceaseless quest for the elusive "Holy Grail" "out there." We assume that when it is acquired or experienced, all will be well. Thus we spend our lives in the futile search for that which can only be found within.

Russell Conwell's classic essay, "Acres of Diamonds," addresses itself to this very problem. He tells of a South African farmer who worked for years on a spread of extremely rocky soil that yielded only the most meager of crops. He would pick up pieces of large rock and curse them as he threw them aside. Finally, in despair, he sold his place for a pittance and left to find greener pastures elsewhere. Many years later he returned to discover that what had once been his farm had become the Kimberley Diamond Mines, the richest plot of ground in all the world. And those rocks that had so hampered his farming were actually huge diamonds in the rough.

"The place on which you are standing is holy ground" (Ex. 3:5). Wherever you are, you are in the center of the divine flow. The great need is to take time to get

yourself centered in it. If you review all the commandments up to this point, you will discover that they all deal with the distractions that lure us away from our center ... and with ways by which we can return. They all lead back to the first commandment, *"You shall have no other gods before me."* You are one in the One. And, in this center within you, you have access to all there is in God.

It is strange how persons on the spiritual quest are often deluded with the belief that the great awakening will be experienced "out there." The tendency is to run off to shrines and holy places and masters, seeking to find the ultimate of spiritual achievement. The old hymn sings, "Not somewhere else, but where thou art." The flow of Spirit is nowhere if it is not in you. You must become your own guru and release your own divine fire.

An extremely important key to dealing with covetousness is appreciation. Appreciate what you have and what you are. This does not mean to become self-satisfied. Divine discontent is a fundamental of human nature. To become satisfied with oneself is to block the divine flow. But there must be self-acceptance. Accept what you are and where you are as the best and only starting points from which to go forward to express the more that is in you.

Plato says that the grateful heart is the great heart that eventually attracts to itself great things. Count your blessings! Consider what you have and ponder how much you might strive for it if you did not have it. Then realize how truly fortunate you are. Stir up the attitude of gratitude which is imperative to keep centered in the flow.

Appreciate people for what they are and for what they have. Instead of letting your mind run to jealousy and envy over what they are and have, acknowledge that they are in the flow. Be grateful that they are demonstrating that there is a flow, and that it is manifesting in them as it can do in you. When you see things in the world that interest you and excite you—the houses, cars, jewels and relationships—experience them instead of coveting them.

A man regularly passed a store on Madison Avenue on his walk to work. One day there was a beautiful painting in the window that caught his eye. He was absolutely struck by it. Every day for many weeks he would stop in front of the store to admire this work of art. It became a highlight of his day. Then one morning the painting was not in the window. It was a shock. He went in to inquire, and he discovered that it was about to be sold. However, the owner gave him an opportunity to purchase it, which he did. He took it home, feeling ecstatic with his new treasure. But where to display it? For weeks he tried the painting on various walls and in various settings. Somehow it was out of place. It just did not fit. In time he came to resist it. All the enjoyment that he had received from it was gone, so he made a decision. He would dispose of it. However, he could not bring himself to sell it. He donated it to an art gallery, which was so delighted to have this classic painting that it was given a lovely setting. Now the man goes often to the gallery to see this work of art with great appreciation.

Carlyle says that wealth is the number of things one loves and blesses and by which one is loved and blessed. It is a good slide rule by which to determine how rich you are: All that you love and bless (not covet) and all that actually blesses you. Actually, the greatest riches may not be in your vault at all. If you love and bless the sunset and feel blessed by it, it is yours, along with parks in the spring, the moonlit night, and the glamorous displays on Fifth Avenue. How rich you are if you can only appreciate life!

If there is something that you have been yearning for, make room in your consciousness for it. Accept it. Experience it. Claim it as yours, not to possess but to enjoy, to bless, and be blessed by. When we turn the word covet inside out, we begin to covet the divine flow, seeking it with all our hearts, minds and souls ... and we are filled. And the first and most important filling is gratefulness. We are full of greatness, full of gratitude.

Then we are ready, perhaps for the first time, to expand our awareness of life to include the whole. Gibran says that this is what prayer is, the expansion of oneself into the living ethers. Suddenly, we can let go our hungers for this and that and just rejoice that *"all that the Father has is mine"* (Jn. 16:15). And then we can know for ourselves:

"I live in this great world and it lives in me. I look out on all that I can see 'northward and southward and east-ward and westward' and I claim it as mine. Not mine to possess, but mine to experience, to bless and be blessed by. I rejoice that I am alive and living in the divine flow. I am grateful, truly grateful, for all the abundance that is mine."

We come to the end of our study ... but every end is a beginning. The Ten Commandments are commended to you for study and reflection. However, the weight of Judeo-Christian tradition notwithstanding, do not keep them. Break the code and find the keys to personal power. I have offered some clues. You will find others. It will be significant only if you make a commitment to work for the changes of consciousness that each commandment suggests.

About the Author

Eric Butterworth was the minister of Unity Center of Practical Christianity in New York City for more than 35 years. He conducted a program of public lectures, growth workshops and retreats, and his radio broadcasts were heard in four states.

Ordained in 1948, he played a vital role in the organization of the present Unity Worldwide Ministries (Association of Unity Churches International). He served churches in Kansas City, Pittsburgh and Detroit and was considered to be one of the leading spokespersons and thinkers in both the Unity and New Thought movements.

He was a frequent contributor to *Unity Magazine*®. Besides his many popular Unity recordings, he published numerous books with Unity, including *In the Flow of Life, Unity: A Quest for Truth, Celebrate Yourself!, The Concentric Perspective* and *Spiritual Economics.*

Mr. Butterworth was born in Canada in 1916 and raised in California. Since his mother was a Unity minister, he grew up with Unity beliefs. He said, "It seems natural to devote my life to the work of helping other people find the influence of Truth in their lives as I have known it in mine."

Eric Butterworth made his transition on April 17, 2003.

B0041